T0079289

Paganism: A Very Short Introduction

VERY SHORT INTRODUCTIONS are for anyone wanting a stimulating and accessible way into a new subject. They are written by experts, and have been translated into more than 45 different languages.

The series began in 1995, and now covers a wide variety of topics in every discipline. The VSI library now contains over 500 volumes—a Very Short Introduction to everything from Psychology and Philosophy of Science to American History and Relativity—and continues to grow in every subject area.

Titles in the series include the following:

Owen Davies

PAGANISM

A Very Short Introduction

OXFORD
UNIVERSITY PRESS

OXFORD

UNIVERSITY PRESS

Great Clarendon Street, Oxford OX2 6DP

Oxford University Press is a department of the University of Oxford.
It furthers the University's objective of excellence in research, scholarship,
and education by publishing worldwide in

Oxford New York

Auckland Cape Town Dar es Salaam Hong Kong Karachi
Kuala Lumpur Madrid Melbourne Mexico City Nairobi
New Delhi Shanghai Taipei Toronto

With offices in

Argentina Austria Brazil Chile Czech Republic France Greece
Guatemala Hungary Italy Japan Poland Portugal Singapore
South Korea Switzerland Thailand Turkey Ukraine Vietnam

Oxford is a registered trade mark of Oxford University Press
in the UK and in certain other countries

Published in the United States
by Oxford University Press Inc., New York

© Owen Davies 2011

The moral rights of the author have been asserted
Database right Oxford University Press (maker)

First published 2011

British Library Cataloguing in Publication Data

Data available

Library of Congress Cataloging in Publication Data

Data available

Typeset by SPI Publisher Services, Pondicherry, India
Printed and bound by
CPI Group (UK) Ltd, Croydon, CR0 4YY

ISBN 978-0-19-923516-2

Contents

List of illustrations

Introduction: defining paganism

It is crucial to stress right from the start that until the 20th century people did not call themselves pagans to describe the religion they practised. The notion of paganism, as it is generally understood today, was created by the early Christian Church. It was a label that Christians applied to others, one of the antitheses that were central to the process of Christian self-definition. As such, throughout history it was generally used in a derogatory sense. So, until the final chapter, this *Very Short Introduction* will largely be looking at paganism through the eyes of the Christian world, and how, over the centuries, notions and representations of its nature were shaped by religious conflict, power struggles, colonialism, and scholarship. In short, this is an introduction to the *idea* of paganism over the last two millennia.

The people who were labelled as pagans in the past followed a hugely diverse array of religious rituals and beliefs. With the exception of the authors of ancient Rome and Greece, though, our knowledge of what they were like is based largely on the Christian clergy. What we know of the religion of the Vikings before their conversion to Christianity, or of the tribes in colonial South America and Africa, for example, has been shaped by the prejudices and agendas of those attempting to impose a new religion upon them. Many of the sources were written retrospectively, decades and centuries after pagan cultures had been Christianized. There are also many gaps in the literary record, and our understanding of religions in some regions in the pre-Christian past relies exclusively on trying to identify and interpret ritual activity from archaeological excavations. In sum, to understand the history of paganism is to recognize the fragmentary, distorted, and partial nature of the sources.

Early origins

Considering what has just been said, it is not surprising that the origin of the word has attracted considerable scholarly debate. The earliest definition of *paganus*, the Latin word from which pagan derives, pertained to 'rustic', 'of the countryside'. From the 5th century onwards, Christian authors began to reframe it in overtly religious terms, describing the *pagani* as rural idol worshippers. Much later, 'pagan' was often translated as 'peasant' in the English language. The overt religious connotations disappeared but the derogatory sense of an ignorant, backward rural dweller continued. These usages gave Christians rhetorical advantage, reinforcing the simple equation that the *'pagani'* were country folk who clung longest to idolatrous non-Christian practices, in contrast with the Christianized urban populations of the Roman Empire. One initial problem with this definition is that organized resistance to Christianity was actually strongest in the cities.

More recent scholarship has reassessed the early use of the term *paganus* in relation to Christianity, and uncovered more nuanced definitions of what it meant. In the 2nd and 3rd centuries AD, a common meaning of *paganus*, as a noun and an adjective, was 'civilian' in the sense of 'non-militant'. This possibly derived from the fact that early Christians referred to themselves as 'enrolled soldiers' of the Christian Church, and so non-Christians were described as *pagani* – those who were civilians and not soldiers of Christ. This definition seems to have become redundant by the 4th century though, and does not provide a satisfactory link with the later development of 'pagan' as explicitly non-Christian.

Another definition, proposed by the French scholar Pierre Chuvin, reconstructs *pagani* as meaning 'people of the place, town, or country, who preserved their local customs'. So in this sense, *pagani* were not backward rural idolaters. They were people defined by the religions of their local communities, whether they be in towns or the countryside. They were the antithesis of *alieni*, or 'people from elsewhere', in other words Christians. It has been pointed out, however, that the etymology of the word does not necessarily equate with its meaning at certain points in time, and that its use in literary documents does not necessarily reflect its use in popular language.

There were other terms used as synonyms for 'pagan' in early Church literature. In the Greek-influenced cultural world of the eastern Mediterranean, the words *ethne* and *ethnikoi* described this category of otherness and foreignness. By the early 4th century, they were superseded by the term *Hellenes*, which referred to those instructed in Greek culture and ideas, and by inference the worship of Greek divinities. 'Barbarian' was another word of Greek origin that would come to be used quite widely. It originally meant someone who did not speak Greek, or who was a foreigner in other words, but it later acquired connotations of cultural if not military inferiority. When it came to spreading the word of the Bible amongst Germanic tribes during the 4th century, the missionary Bishop Ulfilas translated *Hellenes* (Latin *gentilis*) into Gothic as *háithnô*, or 'heathen'. This perhaps denoted, rather like 'pagan', a person who lived in wild remote places (the heaths) and clung to old ways, but it could also derive from the Armenian word *hetanos* for 'nation' or 'tribe'.

The Latin *gentilis*, or 'gentile', can also be found in early Christian and medieval texts. Although today it is used almost exclusively to mean a non-Jew, in the past 'gentile' was used in a Christian context to denote those who were not baptized. So, in his *Etymologiae*, an encyclopaedic summary of all knowledge held at the time, Isidore of Seville (c. AD 560–636) explained that

3

gentiles were those who were 'still in the state in which they were generated, i.e. as they came down into the flesh in sin, serving idols and not yet regenerated'. From the 6th century onwards, 'gentile' became more problematic than 'pagan' due to the increasing influence of the Germanic tribes in western and southern Europe as the Roman Empire crumbled. *Gentilis* had also been used in the sense of a non-Roman 'barbarian', but because by this time many Germanic peoples had also been converted to Christianity, a non-Roman was no longer a non-Christian by definition. Consequently, 'pagan', a word probably in greater popular usage, was increasingly used to clarify the identity of a non-Roman non-Christian.

Isidore's definition of 'gentile' leads us to the issue of how Christians perceived pagans in relation to other competing religions in the Roman Christian world. While 'gentile' could be used in an all-embracing way to refer to all non-baptized people, theologians generally distinguished between pagans, Jews, heretics, and, from the 7th century onwards, Muslims. Yet the boundaries were sometimes deliberately blurred in the Church's pursuit of religious supremacy. We can see this happening in 7th-century Spain. A Church canon, probably dating to around 624, alleged that Jewish parents who were compelled to have their infants baptized were evading the order by hiring the children of Christian neighbours and presenting them for baptism as their own. This way, the Jewish children remained Jews and the Christian children were baptized twice. The pertinent aspect of the canon denounced the Jews for thereby keeping 'their own offspring as pagans by sinister and nefarious pretence'.

Bearing in mind that during the reign of the Visigoth King Sisebut (AD 612–621) there was a virulent royal campaign to eradicate Judaism from Spain through forced conversion and exile, the reference to pagans in this ecclesiastical document can be interpreted as part of a deliberate, political strategy by the Church to undermine the legality of Judaism by demoting it to the illegal status of paganism. In the 15th and 16th centuries, as the Christian monarchy and Church attempted to purge Spain of Moorish influence, a similar stretching of definitions would come to include Muslims.

Later usage

The next major step in the broadening of the political use of paganism occurred during another traumatic European religious conflict – this time between Christians. During the Protestant Reformation of the 16th century, paganism was bandied about as a general term for 'false religions', and for many Protestant theologians there were none more false than Catholicism, with its icons, saint worship, and partaking of Christ's flesh and blood. Rome, once a rock of Christianity in a sea of other 'idolatrous' religions, was now denounced as a see of pagan iniquity.

In his 1624 sermon on *Paganisme and papisme parallel'd*, the Church of England clergyman Thomas Ailesbury likened papal Rome to pagan Rome, describing them as 'folded up into one Masse or Chaos'. He also made an analogy with Jezebel, the ancient biblical queen who led the Hebrews into idolatry. If the Vatican 'were stripped out of those Robes of Paganisme', said Ailesbury, 'she would well-nigh go naked'. For such Protestant theologians, Catholic worship was no better than the practices of the ancient Pagans, which were characterized by sacrifice and sexual immorality. One former Jesuit, Thomas Abernethie, frothed at the mouth with hatred for the 'brutish and Sodomitish life' of the Vatican, which was even 'worse than that of the Pagans'. The 17th-century Genevan minister Pierre Mussard wrote a pamphlet attempting to prove that the Catholic Mass was derived directly from pagan sacrificial rites.

* * *

While over the next few chapters we will move away from defining paganism to looking at the nature of the religions labelled 'pagan' by Christian writers, it must always be borne in mind that the term is problematic, and an awareness of the context in which it was being applied is important. If 'paganism' is so value-laden, so weighed down by prejudice, why continue to use it? Some have tried to avoid it, and have used 'polytheism' instead. As we shall see in the next chapter, though, this also raises interpretive problems. Terms such as 'pre-Christian indigenous religions' could be used, but those religions and belief systems labelled as pagan in the past were not necessarily pre-Christian in origin and not necessarily indigenous.

So pedantic avoidance of 'paganism' can be equally misleading in interpreting the past. Perhaps Frank Trombley, a leading expert on religion in the ancient world, has the right attitude: 'I have discovered no good reason to avoid using the word.' 'If some scholars are troubled about hurting the feelings of generations long past,' he continued, 'I cannot discern any scientific or empirical necessity for such compunction.' Another scholar, an expert on Roman religion, suggests 'one might as well call it that as anything else'. On this note, let us move on to exploring what constituted paganism in the ancient world.

Chapter 1
The ancient world

So if 'paganism' was a product of Christian self-definition, what do we know of the religions that were already in existence before and during the early years of Christianity? Let us begin by considering how far back we can legitimately use the term 'pagan' to define religious activity. Christians did not put a time limit on the age of all the 'other' religions they denounced as pagan, other than that they could only have existed within Old Testament chronology. This takes us back only to around 4,000 BC. But although 'paganism' is an historic concept, as we shall see in later chapters, in modern times anthropologists, folklorists, and neo-pagans pushed back the existence of paganism deep into a prehistoric past that was unknown to human understanding until the last couple of centuries. So a brief overview of prehistory is pertinent.

The earliest religions

Burials are evidence of a conception of an afterlife, and hence notions of a spiritual existence. Examples of deliberate burial amongst modern humans and Neanderthals have been found dating as early as 100,000 BC, though these need not necessarily reflect religious practices. It is in the Upper Palaeolithic (Old Stone Age), roughly between 40,000 and 10,000 years ago, though, that clear evidence of burial *ritual* first appears in the archaeological record. Excavations show that human bones were stained with red ochre, and animal bones, stone tools, and items of adornment such as shells were deliberately placed with the corpse or body parts.

Another likely sign of religious belief in early prehistory relates to carved art objects such as the so-called 'Venus figurines', which have been found at Upper Palaeolithic sites across Europe and Russia. They date to as far back as 35,000 BC, though most are from around 30,000 to 20,000 BC. These carved or moulded female figurines of clay, stone, bone, or ivory, with their emphasized breasts, hips, and belly, have attracted considerable speculation. The general assumption is that they must have some ritual, and therefore presumably religious, significance, most likely related to fertility. It has also been suggested that they are the earliest examples of pornography.

The third main source of evidence for the earliest expressions of religious belief is Upper Palaeolithic cave painting and rock art, such as the world-famous examples from Lascaux and Chauvet in France. The earliest examples have been dated to around 30,000 BC, and mostly depict the animals, such as bison, deer, horses, and birds, that the Palaeolithic artists would have hunted for food. Images of people are exceedingly rare, though. Representations of human identity usually concern body parts such as stencilled hands, heads, and genitals.

These three main sources of archaeological evidence have generated the three main models of our earliest religious beliefs. They are not mutually exclusive. First, there is the notion of the earth mother. It has been argued that the Venus figurines represent a universal mother goddess, the worship of deified fertility. Some believe that echoes of this primal religion can be found in the beliefs and practices of the first Neolithic farmers, and later in the person of the Greek earth goddess Gaia and other female deities worshipped in the ancient world. Second, is the view that the earliest burial practices are indicative of the veneration of the dead, and by extrapolation ancestor worship – that is, the belief that the dead continue to exist in some form and exert an influence over the living. Grave goods are interpreted as providing those in the afterlife with the objects they treasured in life. Distinguishing between acts of commemoration and those of worship in prehistoric archaeological contexts is, however, another source of lively debate. Third, there is animism and associated beliefs.

Animism has often been portrayed as being the most primitive form of religion. This has been largely shaped by 19th-century anthropological and sociological assumptions based on the religious beliefs of what were labelled 'primitive' societies in Africa, Asia, and the Americas. As developed by the influential anthropologist Edward Tylor (1832–1917), to whom we shall return in Chapter 5, animism defined the notion that all elements of the material world, animate and inanimate, were imbued with spirits and were therefore sentient in some form. Rocks, rivers, wind, trees, mountains, and stars were all alike in that they could be communicated with, worshipped, and influenced. There is no concrete archaeological evidence for animism in the Palaeolithic *per se*, but cave and rock art has led to suggestions that their creators were totemistic, that is they believed that the animals they depicted represented the guiding, animistic spirits that watched over them or their family or group, and which were to be worshipped.

The earliest Stone Age religions have also been called 'shamanistic'. Again, this is a term and concept borrowed from 19th- and 20th-century ethnography, and based on the assumption that isolated hunter-gatherer societies in the modern world not only preserved the way of life of humans in the pre-agrarian prehistoric past, but also their animistic spiritual beliefs. The shaman uses narcotic substances or trance techniques to travel to or communicate with the spirit world in order to tap the powers held by the spirits for the benefit of the living. Being members of hunter-gatherer or herding groups, shamans are particularly intimate with animal spirits, and wear pelts and animal headdresses to enhance entry into their realm. The few examples of what appear to be composite creatures – half-human, half-animal – in Palaeolithic art have been interpreted as representing either shamans themselves or the merging of the human spirit with the animal during their trance journeys.

Ancient religions

Mother goddess worship, ancestor worship, and animism are such broad constructs that elements of all three can be found in the religions of the historic world. What distinguishes history from prehistory is, of course, the existence of writing and therefore the literary preservation of beliefs, ideas, and practices. The first known forms of writing, cuneiform pictograms and hieroglyphs on stones and clay tablets, date to the 4th millennium BC. Proper alphabets developed from around 2,000 BC onwards. It is from these early literary records of the Near and Middle Eastern civilizations of Mesopotamia, Babylonia, and Egypt that we get our first clear glimpse of the world of gods and goddesses.

The scholar Leo Oppenheim declared it impossible to write an account of Mesopotamian religion. The evidence, even with the existence of early writing, was insufficient to reconstruct a whole system of belief and worship. Other historians of Mesopotamia have not been put off, though, and the impressionistic picture that emerges from the archaeology shows a highly organized form of religion centred on the ziggurats and their temple complexes. The cuneiform tablets record hymns, myths, and prayers which confirm that the ancient Mesopotamians believed in a pantheon headed by the sky god An, and that the gods were thought to control the heavens, natural phenomena, and the resources of life. So the god Enlil directed the wind that brought the rain. We get firm evidence of the importance of the mother goddess fertility figure in the shape of the deity Ninhursaga. Humans were subservient to the gods and had been created to labour on their behalf. Kings ruled by divine sanction but were still servants. So divining the intentions of the deities was central to Mesopotamian religion and politics.

In general, Mesopotamian kings did not claim to be divine, and the Persians who conquered the region, and far beyond, by the early 5th century BC also maintained the divide between living monarchs and divinity. It was the ancient Egyptians who made their monarchs incarnations of the gods rather than their earthly representatives.

Until the cracking of the hieroglyphs and cuneiform in the 19th century, the history of early religions was dependent on what was written about them by the ancient Greeks and then Romans. Homer's *Odyssey* and *Iliad*, dated to the 8th century BC, provide the first detailed literary account of the social world of the gods, their relationship with mortals, and how, through sacrifice and invocation, the deities were worshipped and why. Under the extraordinary military conquest of Alexander the Great during the 4th century BC, the boundaries of the Greek Empire pushed as far as India to the east and encompassed Egyptian civilization to the south. The Hellenic world that was forged led to an extraordinarily fertile period of intellectual, social, and cultural exchange. Through conquest and trade, the Greeks came into contact with the religions of Asia, the Middle East, Africa, and Mediterranean Europe. Then, during the peak of the Roman Empire in the 1st century AD, Greco-Roman civilization spread across much of Western Europe, providing chroniclers with information about hitherto unknown peoples and religions.

Many forms of religious worship were practised across the Greco-Roman world. There was a state religion officiated by a priesthood, centred on public temples and a liturgical calendar of public worship. This provided an overarching, unifying expression of Roman identity across the Empire. While official religion occasionally embraced non-Greco-Roman influences, the religious worship practised in homes and military camps was extraordinarily diverse, eclectic, and exploratory. At the centre of Roman domestic religion was Vesta, the goddess of the hearth, while the *lares* were minor deities who acted as guardians of the house. There was plenty of room (and rooms) to incorporate non-Roman elements. Syncretism is a term that is often used to describe this process. It refers to the fusion or blending of different religious traditions brought into contact with each other by cultural exchange. So in 4th-century BC Athens, for example, the Thracian moon goddess Bendis was introduced into the Greek pantheon through mercantile and political contacts between the two peoples.

In the Hellenic world, similarities were commonly identified between the gods of different religious traditions, leading to a two-way absorption of deities. The Phoenicians adopted the Greek Poseidon as their sea god. Greeks in Egypt recognized the Egyptian god of creation Amon-Ra as their Zeus and associated Thoth with Hermes. Sometimes deities were adopted because they were both familiar and yet distinctive. The Egyptian goddess Isis, equated with the Roman Ceres and Greek Demeter, fits this model, and she became hugely popular across the Greco-Roman world, with many temples being dedicated to her worship.

The Roman pantheon was, of course, easily exchangeable with the Greek: Aphrodite was Venus, Zeus was Jupiter, and Athena was Minerva, for example. As the Roman Empire expanded, Romans also found some common ground with the gods of the peoples of Western and Central Europe – peoples who were described by the Romans as 'Celts'. When the Romans encountered the religious site of the thermal springs at Bath, England, they recognized the presiding local goddess Sulis as a variant of their own Minerva, and she was subsequently worshipped as Sulis-Minerva. Even if no equations could be found, the veneration of local deities was not deemed offensive to the Roman authorities. The evidence of inscriptions from British Romano-Celtic sites shows that Roman soldiers, who came from across the Empire, made dedications to local Celtic gods, and also to deities from Germanic cultures such as the war god Vheterus and the goddesses known as the Alaisagae.

Syncretism may have been a fundamental unifying aspect of the Greco-Roman world, but when Christians arrived on the scene they did not want to join in. When Christians looked at the religious activity going on around them, at the veneration of ancestors, the deification of nature, the blending of deities, and a pick-and-mix approach to religion, what they saw was paganism. During the first few centuries of the Church, Christian theologians focused on three practices in particular that they saw as defining this false universal religion: polytheism, sacrifice, and idol worship.

Polytheism and monotheism

From the beginning, the early Church considered pagan religions as wholly polytheistic. The worship of multiple deities provided a fundamental demarcation between the monotheisms of Judaism and Christianity and all other religions in the known world: monotheism was the true religion, and all others were false. Today scholars are still using 'paganism' as a synonym for polytheism. The danger is that we describe religions through Judaeo-Christian terminology without showing due awareness that this is the case, and the equation of paganism or pre-Christian religions with polytheism is equally problematic. For one, the term 'polytheism' was coined by the Hellenic Jewish scholar Philo of Alexandria as a means of defining all religions other than Judaism as false. It is also tied to the notion that the move from polytheism to monotheism was a mark of human progress, reinforcing Christian propagandist definitions of paganism as backward and barbaric. It is certainly true that, according to the little evidence we have, pre-Christian religions were by and large polytheistic. Whether they had pantheons of gods like the Romans or localized, nature-based deities, people worshipped different gods for different purposes and at different times and places. Yet we know so little really about the diversity of religious beliefs in illiterate cultures across Europe and the Mediterranean world, that we cannot categorically state that localized monotheistic cults or religions did not exist.

Does the elevation of one god above others that are recognized but not worshipped constitute a form of monotheism? This has been

1. The 'tauroctony', the sun god Mithras sacrificing a bull. This representation was the central icon of the Mithraic mystery religion. The spilling of the blood ensured light and life

argued over regarding the Mithras mystery cult that became popular amongst the Roman military in particular, from the 1st to the 4th centuries AD. Mithras was a sun god and was usually depicted sacrificing a bull. What little we know about the Mithras cult is that he was worshipped in underground sanctuaries where feasting took place. Each sanctuary had a small number of worshippers, between 10 and 36, and in each group there was a hierarchy based on a series of seven initiations. Men moved from one grade to the next until attaining the final stage of perfection and being given the title 'father'. But Mithraism was not strictly monotheistic. Its followers did not exclude other gods in the Roman pantheon, but rather elevated Mithras above all the others.

Its close-knit fraternal nature, membership procedures, and focus on one god have led some to compare Mithraism to the early Christian groups that were also multiplying at the time. One perspective is that the rise of Christianity influenced the generation of a more monotheistic outlook amongst educated Roman society. This found expression in the worship of Helios, the Greek personification of the sun, promoted by the last Pagan Emperor Julian (AD 361–363). Once Christianity had become the official faith of the Roman Empire, and the suppression of non-Christian religions began, pagan apologists began to devise defences of the validity of their faiths, by arguing that, in essence, they and the Christians worshipped one deity. The difference was that they expressed it in different ways.

The idea of the universality of religion was not new by this time. According to the historian and biographer Plutarch (c. AD 46–120):

> There are not different gods for different peoples; not barbarous gods and Greek gods, northern gods and southern gods ... however numerous may be the names by which they are known, so there is but one Intelligence reigning over the world, one Providence which rules it, and the same powers are at work everywhere. Only the names change, as do the forms of worship.

In his novel *The Metamorphoses*, Apuleius (c. AD 125–180) describes the goddess Isis appearing to the story's main character in a dream in which she pronounces, 'I am the single power which the world worships in many shapes, by various cults, under various names.'

Both Plutarch and Apuleius studied at the schools of Athens. It was there that they imbibed the Platonic philosophy that subscribed to this notion of one ultimate divine principle. In the 3rd century AD, the Greek philosopher Plotinus (c. 204–270) founded a new branch of pagan philosophy. It came to be known as Neoplatonism because its followers considered themselves to be heirs to the teachings of Plato and the Platonists of the schools of Athens. Not surprisingly, one of its central religious teachings, put very simply, was that the source of all existence was an entity, the One, who emanated life. Life was an internal spiritual journey on the ascent to be united with the One. Others developed Plotinus's ideas and took them in different directions. A Phoenician philosopher from Tyre (now Lebanon) named Porphyry, for instance, was particularly interested in the buzzing world of spirits or *dæmones* that existed between humans and deity.

Even if in late antiquity it was hardly a widely held religious philosophy, Neoplatonism provided a clear theology for the expression of monotheistic principles, and thereby challenged the exclusivity of the Judaeo-Christian faith. Neoplatonists posed a further problem for Christians in that they did not fit the stereotype of the barbarian or blood-thirsty pagan. Porphyry argued against blood sacrifice and espoused vegetarianism as essential for spiritual health. Neoplatonic philosophy would have a major influence on religious, magical, and scientific thought in the Renaissance world.

If the equation of paganism with polytheism is awkward, then that between Christianity and monotheism is not entirely unproblematic either. One can point, as many have done, to the nature of the Holy Trinity. The worship of saints, which became a key part of popular Christian liturgy, also complicates the emphasis on the reverence of the one God. The medieval Church authorities were at times also concerned with the popular veneration of Mary in this respect. Come the Reformation and Catholics were accused of having elevated the saints to the status of minor deities, and they were denounced as idol worshippers for all the statues and images venerated in churches and shrines.

Sacrifice

In Christian eyes, the practice of blood sacrifice was another fundamental dividing line between their faith and that of the pagans – and the Jews, for that matter. Time and time again in the early Church literature, the point is underlined that Christians had never practised it, and that the only sacrifice they recognized was the ultimate one made by Christ to save humanity. To paint an even bloodier and more barbaric picture of pre-Christian religion, ecclesiasts dredged up examples of how in the centuries before the light shed by their faith, Greeks and Romans had sacrificed humans in honour of Zeus, Diana, Jupiter, Pluto, and Saturn. Christian authorities even denounced the eating of sacrificial animals. The Council of Elvira, convened in Spain in the early 4th century, decreed that Christian landowners should not accept as payment animals and goods that had been dedicated to idols. In 541, the Council of Orléans also ruled that:

> If anyone, after receiving the sacrament of baptism, goes back to
> consuming food immolated to demons, as though he were going
> back to vomit, if he does not comply with a warning from a priest to
> correct this collusion, he shall be suspended from the Catholic
> communion as punishment for his sacrilege.

What are we to make of the Christian picture of pagan blood offering? Let us begin with the matter of human sacrifice. It was certainly a recurring motif in ancient Greek myth, which is what

Christian theologians often referenced in evidence, but there is no clear proof of the practice in the archaeological record. Apart from a couple of exceptional reports of human sacrifice at moments of state insecurity during the 3rd century BC, when Greek and Gaulish couples were apparently buried alive, it was not a Roman religious practice either. In fact, in pagan Greco-Roman literature human sacrifice was generally understood as characteristic of 'bad religion', the religion of 'superstitious' barbarians. Those they accused of carrying it out lived on the edge of the known world – with the list of culprits growing as the Roman Empire expanded. As early as the 6th century BC, there were stories of the Taurians, a people associated with the Crimea, who sacrificed Greek sailors to their goddess. Then there were the accounts of the Carthaginians in North Africa who sacrificed their male children, and the Celts of Western and Central Europe, of whom the 4th-century BC playwright Sopater remarked, 'Among them it is the custom, whenever they win any success in battle, to sacrifice their captives to the gods.'

Were these Greco-Roman reports any more reliable than the later Christian ones? Excavations in Carthage, Tunisia, and other towns in the region, have uncovered *tophets*, or stone enclosures in which thousands of sealed urns containing the burnt bones of infants were buried. They date to a period stretching between the 8th and 3rd centuries BC. Some of the urns also contained beads, amulets, and bird bones, and the *tophets* were dedicated to the gods Baal and Tanit. These finds would seem to support the ancient literature describing Carthaginian child sacrifice, but other interpretations are possible. The *tophets* might just be a cemetery for infants who died from illness and whose afterlives were dedicated to the gods.

As to the Celts, Roman authors told of sacred groves in Gaul sprinkled with human blood and containing heaps of sacrificial human remains. The druids were singled out as the priests of such barbarity, and the image of the druidic wicker man, mentioned by

Caesar, filled with humans ready to be immolated to the gods, remains iconic today. Once again, though, the archaeology is by no means conclusive. The English bog body known as Lindow Man has attracted a great deal of debate in this respect. Some time in the 1st century AD, he received lethal blows to the head, and his jugular vein was cut. His naked body was placed face down in a shallow pool in a marsh in Cheshire. A thong made of animal sinew found around his neck has been interpreted as a garrotte by some, but merely a neck ornament by others. A sacrifice to Iron Age gods? Not necessarily. It is just as likely that he was the victim of a ritualized killing, which is not necessarily the same thing as human sacrifice. Lindow Man could have been a murderer, or have committed some other vile crime, with the circumstances of his death and treatment of his corpse reflecting notions of the spirit world. Maybe he was nothing more than the victim of a terrible accident.

The idea that the spirits of evil people returned to plague the living was widespread in both pre-Christian and Christian history. There is considerable evidence that the bodies of some criminals were dismembered or mutilated and then buried face down, or pinned or weighed down, sometimes in marginal areas away from the living, in order to prevent the corpse or spirit returning. In London, as late as 1834, the corpse of the brutal murderer and suicide Nicholas Steinberg was laid face down in his grave and his skull smashed with a large mallet to this end.

The tendency to seek archaeological proof for the ancient historic record on human sacrifice can lead to fundamental misinterpretations. The stories of sacrifice need to be understood first and foremost as an aspect of the Greco-Roman process of defining their civilization through identifying a set of unacceptable practices that could be attributed to all the 'others'. That is not to say that human sacrifice was never practised. There are examples from other continents in other times. But the historic sources cannot be relied upon, and the archaeology is open to multiple interpretations.

Paganism

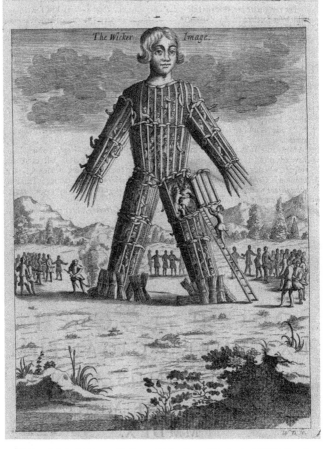

The Wicker Image.

2. From Aylett Sammes, *Britannia Antiqua Illustrata* (1676). Iconic depiction of the wicker man described in Caesar's *Gallic War*, and by the Greek historian and geographer Strabo

There are no such problems with regard to animal sacrifice – the practice was endemic across the known ancient world. It was a unifying form of worship, and concerned the attempt to approach, influence, thank, or propitiate the gods or ancestors. It was also a powerful participatory affirmation of belief. There were two main forms it could take, unconsumed and consumed. So animals could be offered by burning or burying them at sacred spots. This act also represented a personal sacrifice in that the individual, family, or community gave up productive animals without any direct benefit. In contrast, the second form of animal sacrifice concerned ritual feasting on sacrificial animals. There are also examples from Iron Age England, and elsewhere, of a half-way solution. Animals were butchered and then a portion offered up to the gods and the rest ritually eaten. These sacrifices were often great communal as well as religious events, cementing social relations and reinforcing hierarchies. The cultural and political importance of sacrifice is clearly evident from an edict issued in AD 249 by Emperor Trajan Decius. It decreed that all inhabitants in the Empire, no matter what religion, were required to make sacrifice to the gods, eat sacrificial meat, and swear that they had always sacrificed. In short, sacrifice was an act of citizenship.

The animals worthy of offer were generally those that had been domesticated, particularly ones that were bred for food. There are numerous examples of dogs being ritually buried, their skeletons being complete, but they were understandably not popular at ritual feastings. Goats and sheep were commonly sacrificed in Greece, while pigs, sheep, and cattle are often found in ritual contexts in British and French Iron Age sites. Horses were the most precious animals of all, and presumably only sacrificed for exceptional reasons or by high-status individuals. No doubt there were many different localized traditions for which animals were sacrificed, how many, by whom, when, and where. This is certainly apparent in the Hellenic world. At Mount Tithion, Greece, for example, sheep and goats were not sacrificed to Isis, as was common elsewhere, and instead the wealthy offered oxen and deer, and the poor gave up geese and guinea fowl.

Worshipping idols

Christians loved to accuse pagans of idolatry. The Second Commandment ordered: 'You shall not make for yourself any graven image . . . You shall not worship them or serve them.' Put simply, an idol is a physical representation of a god and so an object of worship. In this sense, idolatry was, indeed, central to all religions in the ancient world. In its simplest form, an idol could be a natural feature such as a stone or rock, either unadorned or perhaps partially shaped and decorated. Springs, the givers of life, could also be classed as idols, for they were hugely important sites of veneration associated with deities. There is no better example than the hot springs at Bath, England, which were dedicated to the goddess Sulis-Minerva. Much is found in the written sources regarding the veneration of trees, particularly tall and old ones. In ancient Crete and Greece, the fig tree was sacred, and there are examples where they were worshipped as representing Demeter and Dionysos. Some trees acquired sacred status through their proximity to venerated springs. Theophrastus, the Greek botanist who lived in the 4th and 3rd centuries BC, wrote of a plane tree in Crete, 'next to a spring, which does not lose its leaves. The story goes that Zeus had sex with Europa under this tree.'

The chopping down of such divine trees was a common legend in Christian hagiographies. The prime example is St Martin of Tours, the 4th-century Gaulish bishop, who having demolished an ancient temple in one village set about cutting down a pine tree close by:

> the chief priest of that place, and a crowd of other heathens began to oppose him. And these people, though, under the influence of the Lord, they had been quiet while the temple was being overthrown,

could not patiently allow the tree to be cut down. Martin carefully instructed them that there was nothing sacred in the trunk of a tree, and urged them rather to honour God whom he himself served. He added that there was a moral necessity why that tree should be cut down, because it had been dedicated to a demon.

The Germanic tribes were thought particularly partial to tree worship. According to the Roman chronicler Tacitus (AD 56–117), they rejected the notion of housing their idols in built structures or temples, and believed that trees in their natural environment provided the closest link between humans and the gods.

The Celts too worshipped trees in sacred groves, though apparently they could be artificial creations. In Lowbury, Oxfordshire, it appears that some time in the 1st century AD several trees were planted within a bank and ditch enclosure, in which votive offerings were deposited. They also worshipped wooden posts or columns as abstract representations of sacred trees. In Libenice, Czech Republic, the focal point of a large, 3rd-century BC sacred site was a standing stone and two wooden posts, which had perhaps been carved in human form. Stone pillars, interpretable as representing tree trunks, were also venerated across much of the Mediterranean world. These could be plain or inscribed with symbols and dedications. In Gaul and parts of southern Germany, the influence of Roman culture in the 2nd and 3rd centuries AD inspired the construction of impressive 'Jupiter columns' that reached a height of up to 15 metres. Some featured Jupiter on horseback trampling a giant while others depicted him seated on a throne.

Statues were the most iconic of idols. They could be portable or fixed, wooden or stone. Wood was easier to work and could be sculpted more quickly, but the use of one or the other material was probably mostly dependent on geographical location and cultural and religious tradition. In Europe, stone statuary is largely associated with the Roman and Greek world, and there is no doubt that use of stone spread with the extension of its influence. In southern France, for instance, there was a shift from wooden to stone statuary before the Roman conquest due to the influence of Greek and Roman traders. At the sacred site of Entremont, which was destroyed by the Roman army in 124 BC, the path to the sanctuary was lined with life-size stone statues of men and women.

We have already seen how idols were the focus of sacrifice, but there were other ways to venerate the gods. The lives of animals were not the only gifts that could be sacrificed. Harvested and processed foods were burned or left to decompose at terrestrial sites, or thrown into rivers, pools, and springs. In Greco-Roman worship, libations (drink offerings) of wine were common, most obviously to the wine gods Dionysos and Bacchus but also more generally. Beer, oil, and honey were given too. An ancient Hittite prayer to attract the gods runs: 'See, I have sprinkled your paths, O Telipinu, with sweet oil. So set out, O Telipinu, on the path which has been sprinkled with sweet oil!' The libations might simply be poured on the ground next to or on an idol, or more elaborately presented in special vessels on libation tables.

Intimate personal objects such as jewellery were offered, and although they are rarely preserved in the archaeological record, it is likely hair and clothing were as well. There is a lot of evidence for the sacrifice of valuables. Leaving coins at temple sites was widespread. Numerous coins were found, for example, at a spring dedicated to the goddess Coventina near Hadrian's Wall. At a Romano-Celtic shrine at Brigstock, Northamptonshire, coins had been deliberately placed in the mouths of animal heads. Weapons and other military equipment make up a large proportion of votive offerings, and many examples have been found in wetland and river sites across Europe. One intriguing aspect of such deposits is that the weapons were often apparently deliberately broken or bent, in other words rendered ineffective.

Pagan views of Christianity

The Roman world was full of gossip and rumour about the secret, sordid practices of the Christians, who were considered the followers of a mysterious, uppity Eastern cult. The other religions officially worshipped in the Roman world were generally, though not exclusively, public, with their temples out in the open, their feasts and celebrations inclusive spectacles. Christian worship was portrayed as being secretive, nocturnal, and exclusive. In a dialogue written around AD 200 by a Christian apologist and lawyer named Minucius Felix, the gamut of accusations is described. Christians were 'a people skulking and shunning the light, silent in public, but garrulous in corners. They despise the temples as dead-houses, they reject gods, they laugh at sacred things.' They worshipped the genitals of their priests and the head of an ass. Then there were the stories of incestuous orgies and ritual murder.

> An infant covered over with meal, that it may deceive the unwary, is placed before him who is to be stained with their rites, this infant is slain by the young pupil, who has been urged on as if to harmless blows on the surface of the meal, with dark and secret wounds. Thirstily – O horror! They lick up its blood, eagerly they divide its limbs.

These are the sorts of activities of which Christians would subsequently accuse pagans and Jews, with equally ghoulish relish.

The reason why the Christians attracted such rumours has been mulled over quite extensively. One obvious source of the tales of cannibalism was a misunderstanding of the Eucharist and the transubstantiation of the bread and wine into the flesh and blood of Christ. Then there was the holy kiss. 'Greet all the brethren with a holy kiss' said St Paul. It was easy for this act to attract libidinous rumours. The sacrificial and sexual aspects of anti-Christian propaganda may have also been influenced by the fact that Roman pagans saw Christianity as one of numerous dubious mystery religions from the Near East, some of which also attracted reputations for perversion. There was the Syrian emperor-priest Elagabalus (reigned 218–222) who led worship of the sun god El-Gabal. After his death, he stood accused of coercing followers to engage in depraved sexual excesses. The *Historia Augusta*, an untrustworthy late Roman collection of biographies, states that he sacrificed humans, particularly Italian children of noble birth.

Much closer to the Christian Church in theology were the Gnostic heretic sects that attracted claims of licentious behaviour. One of the better known groups, the Carpocratians, were accused of holding orgiastic love feasts. Then there were the Phibionites who, it was claimed, practised a form of the Eucharist that required the use of menstrual blood and semen. According to the claims of Epiphanius, a 4th-century Church Father, it was crucial that female followers were not impregnated during their sexual worship. If they were, then:

> They pull out the embryo in the time when they can reach it with the hand. They take out this unborn child and in a mortar pound it with a pestle and into this mix honey and pepper and certain other spices and myrrh, in order that it may not nauseate them, and then they come together, all this company of swine and dogs, and each communicates with a finger from the bruised child.

Who knows whether any of these groups were involved in anything close to such activities. What such accounts show, though, is that there was a set of activities that were unacceptable to pagan and Christian alike, and which could be used as propaganda weapons by Romans against Christians, and Christians against non-Christians and heretics.

Chapter 2
Paganism in retreat

The Christianization of the Roman world was a gradual process taking several centuries. As is well known, Constantine the Great (d. AD 337) was the first Roman emperor to adopt Christianity and to give the Church official status in the Empire. The Edict of Milan he instituted in 313 enshrined the freedom of worship for all in the Empire after the persecution of Christians by his predecessor. It was also Constantine who created a new imperial seat in Byzantium (Constantinople), which would become the capital of the Eastern Roman or Byzantine Empire. The shifting power base of the Empire, as its grip in the West began to loosen, was an important influence on the progress of Christianity and so the destiny of the pagan religions of Europe and the Near East.

Legal status

The first prohibition of pagan sacrifice is found in a law code of 341, during the reign of Constans, youngest son of Constantine:

> The madness of sacrifices shall be abolished. For if any man in violation of the law of the sainted Emperor, Our father, and in violation of this command of our Clemency, should dare to perform sacrifices, he shall suffer the infliction of a suitable punishment.

Whether it was specifically directed at pagans is not entirely clear, as it could have equally been directed more generally at soothsaying and other magic practices. It would seem from other sources that the law was not rigorously policed and sacrifice continued in Rome. A further set of laws were issued between 353 and 360 in which the prohibition of sacrifice on pain of death was reinforced and the venerating of pagan images and divination outlawed. The temples were not targeted, as we shall see later.

It was under the reign of Theodosius I (379–395), who, after reuniting the two halves of the old Empire, had became its last ever emperor, that Christianity was made the official state religion. Not surprisingly, he also instituted the harshest legislation yet against paganism. Private and public sacrifice, the decoration of sacred trees, and the raising of turf altars were made treasonable offences. Pagan holidays dedicated to the old gods were decreed normal working days. Yet, although sometimes taken as heralding the end of paganism, the old Roman religions continued to be practised amongst the urban elite and the rural common people. It has been estimated that at the death of Theodosius more than half of the Roman population was still pagan. Still, for ambitious politicians and state functionaries, it was becoming amply clear that being pagan was increasingly unprofitable in career terms.

Over the next century, Theodosius's successors continued to promulgate laws against paganism. Emperor Leo I banned pagans from the legal profession around 468 for instance. But generally there was a degree of religious toleration in the Byzantine Empire of the 5th and early 6th centuries, particularly during the reign of Anastasius (AD 491–518) when it has been estimated that there were more than 30 active religious creeds. Athens, Alexandria, Gaza, and other cities and towns were still centres of Hellenic pagan thought and practice.

A last major purge of paganism was instituted by the Byzantine Emperor Justinian I (ruled 527–565), as part of a wider political and religious policy of imposing orthodox Christianity on his subjects. Pagans were ordered to report to the nearest church, where they were to receive Christian instruction and baptism. The penalty for non-compliance was loss of citizenship and confiscation of property. Baptized Christians found guilty of participating in pagan practices faced the death penalty. Non-Christians were banned from teaching, and the famed schools of Athens, home of classical scholarship, were shut down in 529. The works of the great classical thinkers were devalued. There are also accounts of the prosecution of pagans taking place, such as in Antioch between 554 and 559. Those found guilty were sentenced to work in hospitals, imprisoned in monasteries, or were executed. It should be noted that Justinian's intolerance extended to Christian sects as well as pagans.

Conversion in the West

Through the 5th century, the Western Roman Empire disintegrated under pressure from the Huns and Visigoths. Rome was sacked by the latter in 410, and they subsequently invaded and settled in parts of Gaul and Spain. The Western Empire hung on, with Roman emperors relying on the support of various 'barbarian' armies for their political survival. The Western Empire formally ceased to exist by 480. Considering this history of instability, humiliation, and compromise, it is not surprising that Christianity was politically more difficult to impose than in the Eastern Empire. Indeed, some pagan intellectuals blamed the decline of Rome on the adoption of Christianity. As to the conquering Germanic tribes, it is remarkable that most of the rulers who seized chunks of the old Roman world converted to Christianity within a generation or two. In the process, the contrast that Roman Christians made between their refined culture and that of the barbarian hordes blurred. Could a Christian be a barbarian?

The Roman territories in Iberia and south-western France were seized in the early 5th century by Visigoths who crushed other tribal settlers in the region such as the Alans, who originated from Iran, and the Germanic Vandals. The Visigoth aristocracy had already converted to a non-Roman, 'Arian' form of Christianity inspired by the Egyptian theologian Arius. According to Arius, Jesus was divine but not God. The tensions between Arian and Roman branches of Christianity, the attempts to reconcile them, and the suppression of various schisms, may have distracted the Visigoth rulers from eradicating remnant paganism in Spain. A law code of 506, during the reign of Alaric II, re-enforced anti-pagan and anti-magic legislation throughout Visigoth territories in Spain and France. But it would seem that there was no concerted attempt to enforce the ban on pagan practices for much of the 6th century. At a regional council in 590, bishops condemned the popular custom of holidaying on Thursdays in honour of Jupiter. Writing in the mid-6th century, St Martin of Braga found the Christians in Galicia, a region ruled by the Christian Germanic Sueve between 411 and 584, still observing pagan rites, and dedicated much energy to correcting this state of affairs. Yet, as Church councils held at Toledo at the end of the 7th century indicate, the worship of idols and pre-Christian shrines was still considered problematic. The Toledan Council of 693 ordered that offerings made to sacred trees, springs, and stones must be brought to local churches where they would be exposed as blasphemous superstition before the people. Less than 30 years later, nearly all of Iberia was under Islamic Moorish rule, and it would become a beacon of religious tolerance, with Christians, Jews, and Muslims all having the freedom to worship. By this time, though, pagan faiths had long been vanquished.

In France, there is no convincing evidence that pagan religions existed formally beyond the early 6th century. Thanks to the military leadership of the Germanic Frankish King Clovis (d. 511), by this time much of what we know of as France was under the rule of the Merovingian dynasty. Clovis had married a Christian princess, and subsequently converted to Roman Christianity, probably in the 490s. The sources of the period indicate that the clergy, albeit primarily located in Mediterranean France, encountered only fragmentary non-Christian practices that were considered detached from their original purpose. This is certainly reflected in the writings of bishop Caesarius of Arles (d. 543), one of the key sources for the period. In one of his sermons, he observed that:

> Some people, through either simplicity or ignorance or, what is certainly more likely, gluttony, do not fear or blush to eat of that impious food and those wicked sacrifices which are still offered according to the customs of the pagans.

The repeated ecclesiastical expressions of concern about such customary activities in Merovingian Gaul were probably inspired as much by an anxious awareness of pagan kingdoms to the north and east in Germanic lands, as by concern over their pernicious continuance amongst practising Christians in Gaul. The threat from the North will be discussed in the next chapter.

Across the Channel, in England, organized paganism seems to have survived longer, though there are few details about the nature of pagan worship in Anglo-Saxon ecclesiastical documents. Augustine had founded the archbishopric of Canterbury in 597, and in 601 he baptized the first royal convert, King Æthelberht of Kent. According to the early 8th-century monk and chronicler Bede, whose *Ecclesiastical History of the English People* is the main source of information for the Christianization of England, Eorcenberht (d. 664) of Kent was the first king to order that pagan idols be destroyed and so actively to enforce Christianity. According to Bede, the last pagan kingdoms of Sussex and the Isle of Wight were converted in the 680s. Bede, who died in 735, clearly considered paganism to have been eradicated by his day, and there is no clear evidence in other documents of the 8th century that pre-Christian practices were a major problem. That does not mean they did not continue, but the paucity of explicit condemnations in canons and edicts demonstrates that there were no pockets of organized resistance to the Church by this time.

So by the 8th century across nearly all the former territories of the Roman Empire, non-Christian religions had been expunged. How was this achieved? It was one thing for emperors and popes to issue decrees and edicts and another to enact them successfully across thousands of miles of territory.

How to convert pagans

The first step in the conversion process was to send out missionaries into the heart of the pagan territories, ideally to live amongst them. If they were to be successful though, they had to concentrate on influencing the ruling elites. The motive for pagan rulers to convert was undoubtedly political as much as spiritual. That said, successes in battle after having undergone conversion no doubt bolstered personal faith in the new religion. Blandishments and enticements further helped the process. Take Edwin of Northumbria, for example, who was baptized at York in 627. Pope Boniface V sent him two personal letters requesting that he renounce paganism, and gifts of fine gold-embroidered apparel demonstrated the wealth of Christian largesse. Edwin's wife Æthelburh was also offered a silver mirror and an ivory comb decorated with gold. She was half-Merovingian and a Christian. This scenario of royal conversion following marriage to a Christian wife was repeated quite a few times in the annals of Christianization.

Once a state had officially turned Christian, the next major step was the establishment of a permanent physical presence. Taxes and rents raised from newly converted peoples helped fund the building of churches and monasteries. The subsequent accumulation of land generated further wealth. It is impossible to give precise figures for the number of early Christian religious

3. A 15th-century illustration of St Dymphna, a legendary 7th-century Irish princess who was martyred for resisting the incestuous advances of her pagan father. The story originated in the 11th century

establishments that were created in the first few centuries of the Church. In Egypt, around 50 to 60 possible Coptic sites have been identified, while 450 Byzantine churches have been recorded in Palestine. By AD 600, around 100 monasteries and convents existed in Italy and over 200 in Gaul, mostly along the Mediterranean coast. The early monasteries were important as bases for missionary work, as social welfare organizations, educational centres, and occasionally as detention centres.

The role of monks in the conversion process varied. In some cases and places, as we shall see, they acted as Christian 'shock troops' sent to destroy shrines and pagan places of worship. More generally, they were evangelizers preaching the Christian message and baptizing the rural populace. There were a variety of obstacles to their work. Lack of familiarity was one barrier. Many monks were not from the areas or cultures in which they toiled. Martin of Braga, founder of several monasteries in the Galician region of Spain and northern Portugal, and patient evangelizer in the region, was from the Roman province of Pannonia in south-eastern Europe. Irish missionaries travelled far and wide. Bede captures some of the trepidation they must have felt when he wrote how Augustine and his fellow monks set off for Britain: 'Then they began to feel alarmed and dread the journey, and thought it would be wise and safer to return home, than to visit a barbarous and savage race of unbelievers, whose very language was strange.'

The success of conversion was enhanced if the missionaries were related ethnically to the peoples they were trying to convert, and even more crucially if they knew the languages they spoke, bearing in mind that many languages in Europe had no written form. Bishop Ulfila is the classic example of the importance of these qualities. Ulfila was the son of a Goth and a Cappadocian (from part of Turkey), and was fluent in Greek, Latin, and Gothic. He was consecrated as a bishop in 341 and then spent seven years preaching Arian Christianity amongst the Goths in Dacia, a province now in modern Bulgaria. Due to a bout of Christian

34

persecution, Ulfila led a band of Christian Goths back across the Danube into Roman territory, where they settled near the town of Nicopolis (also in modern Bulgaria). Ulfila's lasting achievement was the translation of the Greek Bible into Gothic, which required the creation of a new alphabet.

There were also physical obstacles to communicating with many isolated rural settlements, particularly in mountainous areas. Then there were the transhumant populations of pagan pastoralists and nomads who were not permanently settled and therefore with whom it was difficult to have a conversionary dialogue. Within communities and families, there were intergenerational challenges as well. Educating a new generation of Christians was easier than converting adults who had been brought up in a non-Christian faith, and whose modes of worship were engrained in their ways of thinking and acting.

One way of breaking the ritual pagan rhythms of a community was to obstruct the physical act of worship. In the Roman world, where paganism was highly institutionalized, this meant dealing with the temple buildings where people placed their votive offerings. There are examples of major temple sites being destroyed by Christian authorities. In 402, for instance, an imperial decree was obtained for the obliteration of pagan temples in Gaza, amongst them those dedicated to Hecate, Aphrodite, Apollo, and Zeus. Yet there was no great wave of state-sponsored destruction that crashed across the Christian world. The destruction of temples was not mentioned in the early decrees against paganism. In fact, there are several that ordered them to be preserved in certain situations. An imperial decree issued in 342 required that rural temples outside the walls of Rome be maintained:

> For since certain plays or spectacles of the circus or contest derive their origin from some of these temples such structures shall not be torn down, since from them is provided the regular performance of long established amusements for the Roman people.

That said, in areas more distant from central authority, particularly in Africa, it is the case that local bishops and monks instigated their own exercises in temple demolition. The archaeology suggests, though, that overall Christians destroyed comparatively few temples.

The idols, images, and physical objects of pagan worship contained in the temples and shrines were another matter. They had no function worth preserving, other than an aesthetic value in the case of high-quality sculptures. The desecration and destruction of idols and images was a dramatic, theatrical act demonstrating the power of Christianity over the old gods. The Coptic monks in Egypt were particularly zealous in this respect. The hagiography of Abbot Shenoute (AD 348–465), whose monastery was situated in the desert near Thebes, describes how on one occasion he came into a pagan village, 'entered the temple and smashed the idols which had been cast down one after the other'. On another occasion, he, along with some fellow monks, entered a shrine containing idols, 'picked them up, took them down to the river, smashed them in pieces and threw them in the river'. In 489, the monks of Tabennesi trashed the Isis cult of Menouthis, and burned many of the images and idols they found in front of local people. Some were brought to Alexandria and placed in a public square where they were displayed for public ridicule.

Sacred groves and trees were also an easy target. The biographer of St Hypatius recorded how he went about conversion in Bithynia (in northern Turkey):

> If he heard that there was a tree or some such which people worshipped, he went there at once taking along his disciples the monks, cut it down, and burned it. Thus they became Christians in part.

Another hagiography, that of St Nicholas of Sion, refers to a village in southern Turkey where the men complained about an ancient cypress tree, 80 feet tall, in which an 'unclean idol' dwelt. When the villagers refused to chop it down, monks from the local monastery came to fell it.

Violence, confrontation, and demolition were by no means the dominant impulses, though. Incorporation and assimilation were also effective long-term policies. A letter dated 601 from Pope Gregory I to Bishop Mellitus, who was preparing to join Augustine of Canterbury's mission to England, is the classic statement of this strategy:

> Tell Augustine that he should by no means destroy the temples of the gods but rather the idols within those temples. Let him, after he has purified them with holy water, place altars and relics of the saints in them ... Further, since it has been their custom to slaughter oxen in sacrifice, they should receive some solemnity in exchange. Let them therefore, on the day of the dedication of their churches, or on the feast of the martyrs whose relics are preserved in them, build themselves huts around their one-time temples and celebrate the occasion with religious feasting. They will sacrifice and eat the animals not any more as an offering to the devil, but for the glory of God.

St Nicholas of Sion adopted a similar policy in early 6th-century Turkey. He and his monks allowed for feasting and the sacrifice of seven calves to take place as part of Christian celebrations at rural chapels. Missionaries in 9th-century Sweden were also prepared to enter a dialogue with Viking pagans regarding the adoption of Christ into their pantheon.

There are numerous Greek examples of the conversion of temples into churches from the 5th century onwards. An early example is the Asklepieion on the slopes of the Akropolis in Athens where a Christian basilica, or large church, was built on the top of a ruined pagan sanctuary. In the late 5th century, a church was built in the famed sanctuary of Delphi, and an inscription of the same period refers to a temple dedicated to Athena having been converted into a Church of the Virgin Mary. At the Roman town of Thuburbo Maius in Tunisia, a temple complex dedicated to Tanit and Baal was converted into a church, likewise a Mithra temple in Alexandria, Egypt. Some of these early churches bear triumphant inscriptions recording the transformation of once pagan sites. An early 6th-century church dedicated to St George in Ezraa, Syria, has an inscription that begins:

> The gathering place of demons has become the house of God,
> Saving light has illuminated where darkness concealed, Where
> [there were] sacrifices of idols, now [there are] choirs of angels.

Another church in the city of the same date has one that records,

> For this house was formerly made of sculpted demons, built
> with useless stones.

It is important to stress, though, that in most cases it would seem that churches were built at such pagan sites long after they had been abandoned and pagan worship had ceased. In other words, they do not represent a systematic policy of hostile and immediate appropriation of sacred spaces.

In cities and major towns, the building of some churches on former temple sites can be put down to land pressure. Derelict, decaying temples represented what would be advertised today as prime location brown-field sites. Another reason for siting churches on or next to pre-Christian monuments, particularly in rural areas, is that former sacred spaces retained their popular significance decades and centuries after their original religious function had ceased. This is clear from the historic use of prehistoric monuments in the English landscape. Neolithic and Bronze Age burial mounds continued to be the focus of religious and spiritual activity 2,000 years and more after their construction. Roman and Anglo-Saxon burials have been found inserted into and around them, and graves from the same periods were also deliberately created in or around other prehistoric monuments such as Neolithic henges. There was no cultural or ancestral link between the builders of these monuments and those who interacted with them two millennia later. Yet these ancient features in the landscape were identified as being artificial monuments, built by gods, supernatural beings, or imaginary ancestors, and consequently were deemed special places for faith activities by early Christians as well as their pagan predecessors. The impressive example of Knowlton Church, Dorset, which is situated within a 5,000-year-old henge monument, is a good, though unusual, case in point. The church was built in the 12th century, therefore long after the area had been Christianized. There is no evidence for an earlier structure. It is usually cited as representing the Christianizing of a pagan monument or as symbolizing the 'transition from pagan to Christian worship'. But it is better understood as illustrating the profound significance of the landscape as a record of memory and the root of popular worship whether pagan or Christian.

Continuance of paganism

Pagan worship continued well into the second half of the first millennium in parts of the eastern Mediterranean world that were officially Christian or subsequently Islamic. Simeon Stylites the Younger (d. 597) encountered pagan villagers and their groves and idols in the Syrian countryside around the great city of Antioch. The thousands of 5th- and 6th-century lamps found in caves dedicated to Pan and Apollo in the Attica mountains, around Athens, suggest the continuance of old pre-Christian practices that had formally been abandoned two centuries earlier. In the 'blessed city' of Edessa, there is evidence that communities of pagans were organizing sacrifices to Zeus-Hadad in the late 6th century.

Pagans and Christians co-existed in Athens into the 6th century, and early Christian basilicas and pagan temples stood in proximity to each other in other Greek cities. Despite the restrictions on pagan worship, it has been suggested that between 395 and 491 at least twelve pagan civil servants worked in the Byzantine bureaucracy. Furthermore, urban pagans could have slipped into the countryside to worship. Perhaps the most remarkable example of co-existence was the religious centre at Philae, an island in the Nile in southern Egypt. Although under the jurisdiction of the Roman-Byzantine Empire, and so its various edicts suppressing paganism, the formal worship of Isis continued there until 537, a date that is generally accepted as marking the formal end of Ancient Egyptian religion. Inscriptions and a papyrus document show that for at least a hundred years Christian officials and priests of Isis existed together on the island. The building of the Church of St Stephen at Philae was not necessarily an aggressive anti-pagan act marking the closing of the temple, and it has been suggested that the worship of Isis could have continued on the island after it had been built.

The city of Harran (Carrhae) provides the most striking and intriguing example of the survival of a pagan community. Located on the border between Turkey and Syria, and founded as a trading post along routes connecting the eastern Mediterranean with Mesopotamia, Persia, and beyond, Harran was part of the Roman Empire during late antiquity and nearby Edessa was a major centre of Christianity in the region. Despite these hampering influences, paganism continued to flourish there, co-existing with a small Christian community. The exact nature of the 'old faith' of the pagans of Harran, as one early Christian source called it, is difficult to decipher. Hellenistic Neoplatonic philosophy was certainly an influential component, and Mesopotamian and Syrian deities were worshipped. Those named include Bath Nikkal, Bar Nemre, Sin, and Gadlat. Worship of planetary gods, the moon in particular, was clearly important. The problem is that despite the archaeologically rich evidence of Syrian pagan temples, very little is known about the religion that inspired them. Harran surrendered peacefully to Arab Islamic forces around 640, and while Christian and Muslim sources on Harran in the centuries that followed are scant, sketchy, and contradictory, the indication is that some form of paganism continued to be tolerated for a further couple of centuries.

As to episodes of reversion back to paganism, there are a few short-lived examples, most notably and influentially that of Emperor Julian in 360–363, the last pagan ruler of the Roman Empire. A lukewarm Christian at best, he renounced his baptism and proclaimed he was guided and protected by Zeus. He ordered the rebuilding of temples, the restoration of old ceremonies and the invention of new ones, and, most repugnant of all to Christians, espoused the practice of blood sacrifice, mostly involving birds. The extent to which this brief restoration influenced far-flung corners of the crumbling Empire is difficult to gauge, though it has been suggested that some sign of it can be detected in the Romano-British archaeological record. Staying in England, but moving forward three centuries, Bede related that some Christians reverted to pagan worship following a visitation of the plague. In 664, King Sigehere of Essex 'began to restore the derelict temples and to worship images', presumably because the new faith had been deemed an inadequate protection against the pestilence. A bishop was dispatched from the neighbouring kingdom of Mercia to restore the faith.

Archaeological evidence

I have referred here and there to the archaeological evidence, which can fill in some of the many gaps in the fragmentary story of pagan survival provided by the written record. The archaeology can also be easily misinterpreted, though. There has been considerable debate, for instance, about the interpretation of burials. Over 100,000 graves dating to the period between AD 450 and 1,000 have been excavated, providing perhaps the most valuable resource we have about the religious world of low-status people living during this time. Archaeologists have long used graves as a measure of the continuance of paganism and the spread of Christianity. It was assumed that the placement of goods in Christian-era burials was evidence of pre-Christian practices. Likewise, the presence of artefacts bearing Christian iconography in graves was taken as conclusive evidence of the Christian faith of the deceased. These basic assumptions are now largely discredited, as is the simplistic interpretation of all east–west burials as Christian. This alignment is also evident in pre-Christian Scandinavia and elsewhere.

It is now clear that the early church in the West tolerated the placement of grave goods. In the Frankish kingdoms, lavish grave depositions have been found inside churches, and the practice seems to have become more popular after the adoption of Christianity by their royalty. Doubt has also been cast on the interpretation of furnished burials as representing residual pagan beliefs about the afterlife, as numerous ethnographic examples have been found where burial goods have no link to concepts of post-mortem existence. As to the presence of Christian iconography in burial deposits, it has been argued that the presence of cruciform jewellery could be reflective of the adoption of Mediterranean fashions rather than Christian theology.

Did paganism disappear?

This is a deliberately dubious question. It is true that all the peoples we have been discussing in this chapter were nominally Christian. Rulers had adopted the faith, their pagan subjects had been baptized, and the churches controlled their formal religious worship. This much we know. But what we know far less about is the extent to which individuals, families, and communities thought and behaved like devout Christians. At what point did people stop thinking of the old gods, cease invoking and propitiating them in private? Did it take decades or centuries?

What we are often left with in the archaeological and written records are impressions of pagan practices in the Christian era that are not necessarily pagan. There is a danger of assuming that at a popular level, Christianity was merely a veneer over continuing pre-Christian patterns of worship. There is evidence that some pagan elements were Christianized. But claims that people were wilfully venerating pagan gods a couple of centuries after the formal adoption of Christianity, in whatever kingdom, are difficult to substantiate.

Furthermore, one of the reasons Christianity was adopted so easily is that it provided its own set of similar notions and practices which served familiar functions to those of pagan religions – as one might expect from a religion that developed in the multi-faith environment of the Roman Empire. A degree of syncreticism was bound to occur on the ground. We can learn from the history of how Protestantism was introduced and adopted in the 16th century, for which we have vastly greater source material. The Protestant Churches' attempt to suppress Catholic practices, such as the veneration of saints and the celebration of the Catholic ritual year, was difficult enough, but making people think like good Protestants was even harder. People could in most respects be good practising Protestants but still commemorate All Saints' Day, or request exorcisms without necessarily considering them explicitly Catholic actions. Reformation historians talk of a 'long Reformation' to describe this experience, and likewise, it seems appropriate to talk of a 'long conversion' regarding paganism.

Paganism also became subsumed, even lost, within the broad categories of superstition and magic. From the 4th century, Christian authorities frequently used the Latin term *superstitio*, from which 'superstition' derives, as a synonym for paganism. It had been in use for centuries, employed in the earliest Latin texts to describe the divinatory practices of non-Roman religions, before becoming a more all-embracing, derogatory word for the religious worship of 'other' cultures, denoting a degree of excessive fear or credulity regarding deities. It was applied to the early Christians and the magic they were accused of practising. With Christianity the dominant religion, the tables were turned, and so *superstitio* became synonymous with 'false' non-Christian beliefs. The term became more ambiguous in that it described both pagan practices and magic: the two were conflated and, from the 6th century onwards, the campaign against the vestiges of paganism became a war on superstition.

The most influential theologian in shaping this redefinition was St Augustine of Hippo (not to be confused with Augustine of Canterbury). Born in Roman North Africa in 354 to a Christian woman, he was initially drawn to unorthodox philosophies including Neoplatonism, and was only baptized in 387 while studying and teaching in Milan. On returning to his homeland, his influence grew quickly and he was ordained bishop of Hippo Regius, a town located in modern Algeria. In a series of works, *On Christian Theology*, *City of God*, and *On the Divination of Demons*, he explored at great length how and why pagan rites were 'superstitious'. He argued, moreover, that the gods worshipped by the pagans were, in fact, Satan's demons in disguise. So the worship of idols, the resort to divination, the wearing of protective amulets, and the like, were essentially pacts with the Devil. Augustine's demonizing of paganism, and the categorization of magic as diabolic, would come to define the Christian conception of witchcraft and magic – with profound consequences.

Chapter 3
Gods in the North

As noted in the last chapter, the leaders of some Germanic tribes had converted as early as the 4th century, but it was in northern Europe that non-Christian religions held out the longest against the spread of Christianity. The obvious reason for this is that the region lay outside the Roman Empire, but the story is more complicated than that, with cultural, political, and geographical factors all playing their part. The fate of paganism in much of northern Europe, excluding Scandinavia, was determined, in particular, by the rise of the Franks under the leadership of Charlemagne (742–814), and the subsequent formation of the Holy Roman Empire which united much of Europe for the first time since the Romans. Charlemagne's forging of his Frankish Carolingian Empire was promoted as a great Catholic endeavour, and as never before the suppression of paganism became a militaristic exercise.

Saxons

By the mid-8th century, nearly all the powerful peoples of Western Europe, the Franks, the Anglo-Saxons, and the Burgundians of eastern France, had converted to Christianity. The Saxons, a grouping of tribes in what is now north-west Germany, were the last to hold out. Our understanding of their religious beliefs is clouded by problems with the few sources we have. The work of the 9th-century monk Rudolf of Fulda, from a Benedictine monastery founded in central Germany in 744, is a key text. The problem is that his account of the history and beliefs of the Saxons borrow heavily from Tacitus's *Germania*, an ethnographic account of the peoples north of the Roman Empire written in the late 1st or early 2nd century AD, and from various Carolingian texts, most notably Einhard's *Life of Charlemagne*. So, the material is ancient, indirect, or from the victors' quill. Alarm bells ring when Rudolf states that the Saxons came from Britain. As to Saxon religion, Rudolf's account is heavily based on *Germania*, which can hardly be taken as representative of peoples in the region seven centuries later. One of the few insightful observations made by Fulda was that:

> They worshipped as divine the trunk of a tree of no small size, set on high, calling it in their own language Irminsul, which in Latin means universal column, as if it holds everything up.

A rare reference to Saxon deities comes from a late 8th-century baptismal creed, one of the few Old Saxon documents that survive from the period, in which the convert is required to state: 'I forsake all the works and words of the devils, Thunaer and Woden and Saxnote and all the fiends that are their companions.' Thunaer (Thor, Donar) and Woden (Odin) are well-known deities in Germanic and Norse mythology, while Saxnote is obscure, with only one other known reference, and has been translated as 'sword companion' or 'companion of Saxons'.

Otherwise we rely largely on references to paganism amongst the population of neighbouring Hesse as described in the hagiography of St Boniface, which was written by Bishop Willibald around 765. Boniface was born in Britain, possibly Devon, in the late 670s, and received his religious training at the monastery of Adescancastre, Exeter, and at an abbey in the south of England, in what was the kingdom of the West Saxons. In 716, he left on his first, short-lived mission to convert the Frisians – a people

46

whose language was similar to his own Old English. Then, in 719, he was given papal authority to preach the gospel amongst the pagan peoples to the right of the River Rhine. It was in northern Hesse, at a place called Geismar, near the town of Fritzlar, that he and his followers came across a sacred oak tree that was of considerable religious significance in the locality. According to Willibald, it was:

> A certain oak of extraordinary size, which is called, by an old name of the pagans, the Oak of Jupiter [Donar]. And when in the strength of his steadfast heart he had cut the lower notch, there was present a great multitude of pagans, who in their souls were most earnestly cursing the enemy of their gods. But when the fore side of the tree was notched only a little, suddenly the oak's vast bulk, driven by a divine blast from above, crashed to the ground.

Those gathered were duly impressed and began to bless the Lord. Boniface's followers then proceeded to build a small oratory on the spot using the wood of the great oak. While this legend represents a great victory over the pagan mind, and although Boniface founded numerous religious establishments in the region, his mission struggled to root out the old religious beliefs. In his absence while working in Frisia to the north, there was apparently considerable backsliding amongst the converted.

Through military conquest Charlemagne finished what Boniface and his disciples had started, but the Saxons were a major obstacle to the expansion of Charlemagne's Christian empire. He launched a first attack in 772, during which it was reported that his forces cut down an Irminsul near Eresburg, and seized gold and silver votive offerings. During the next couple of years, he turned his attention southwards, conquering the Lombards. He became the first Frankish king to visit Rome. Bavaria was incorporated into the kingdom during the following decade, as Charlemagne pushed further southwards and eastwards. All the time, though, the Saxon tribes remained a thorn in his side. It took another 30 years of annual campaigns to subdue them completely. For Charlemagne, paganism was a source of resistance, and so it was probably political as much as religious that, once in control of Saxon territory, he instituted harsh laws, the *Capitulatio de Partibus Saxoniae* (Capitulary for the Saxon Regions), to suppress it. The death penalty was to be meted out to those who sacrificed to idols, failed to keep a Lenten fast, cremated the dead, or rejected baptism. Punishment was also ordered for witches, soothsayers, and magicians – in other words, those who practised pagan superstition in the eyes of the Church. Summary executions of resistant pagans apparently took place, a policy that disturbed some churchmen.

There were a series of rebellions, though the extent to which they were religiously inspired is difficult to assess. One source of resistance was the pagan Widukind, scion of one of the most powerful Saxon families. His rebellions may, in part, have been provoked by the harsh measures expressed in the *Capitulario*. Still, after military defeat in 785, he finally accepted baptism. As late as 841, another rebellion took place, though this time the peasantry rather than the nobility led it. The *Stellinga*, as they were known, resented what they saw as their enslavement under the Frankish yoke. One chronicle explained that 'They, always inclined to evil, preferred to imitate the rites of the pagans rather than to keep the sacraments of the Christian faith.' The Frankish claims that the *Stellinga* were religiously motivated may have been no more than propaganda, legitimizing action against what may have been solely an issue of feudal taxation.

Moving eastwards

In 792, Charlemagne set his sights on the Avars of Hungary. It was a campaign that was trumpeted as a crusade against the last powerful pagan state in mainland Europe. By the late 6th century, the Avars, led by their ruler, or *Khagan*, had built up a large and powerful presence in central and south-eastern Europe, receiving considerable sums in tribute from the Byzantine Empire to the south. Their power began to wane slowly from the mid-7th century onwards, and they were ripe picking for the Franks.

Although promoted as a war on pagans, the realities on the ground before and after the Frankish success were far more complicated. For one, Christian communities had existed amongst the Avars since the beginning of the 7th century. Furthermore, in the wake of the collapse of the Avar state, various Slavic pagan princes filled the vacuum, such as Prince Pribina and Prince Mojmir of Moravia. They paid obeisance to the Frankish rulers, and allowed Roman Catholic missionaries to spread the gospel, but the Franks did not instigate a great campaign of conversion in the region.

Mojmir and other Moravian princes received baptism in 831, but it would seem that paganism continued to be practised openly in the region decades after this date. The pagan sanctuary at Mikulčice, a Moravian stronghold, remained in use into the second half of the 9th century. At another major site, Pohansko, two pagan shrines dating to the end of the 9th century have been excavated. In the 860s, the missionary priests of Passau were criticized for 'not preventing the holding of sacrifices' in Moravia. Of the deities that were worshipped nothing is known. Perhaps the Moravians shared the same pantheon as other eastern Slavs which included the thunder god Perun, the god of the herd Volos, and the goddess Mokoš. Excavations at Mikulčice revealed the sanctuary to be focused on a pit containing clay statuettes of horses and cattle, and crude human heads.

To the north, the Polabian Slavs, who had settled in what is now eastern Germany in the 7th century, held even more tenaciously to their religion. Only when a large swathe of Polabian territory was under the control of the Carolingian Empire in the 10th century did the missionary campaign begin in earnest, with bishoprics being founded in Brandenburg in 948 and Oldenburg in 968. Neither the political or religious imposition went unchallenged. The religious centre of Brandenburg was trashed in 983 and the clergy slaughtered. Another uprising took place in 1066, during which the Scottish Bishop of Mecklenburg, John Scotus, was captured and later decapitated. His head was offered to the god Svarozhits. It has been suggested that religious rebellion was fuelled by Christianity being closely associated with Frankish aggression, and so the Christian God was considered as a German deity. There may have been good reason. As late as 1245, the monastery of Diesdorf warned several local villages that if they refused to give up their paganism then 'faithful Teutonic Catholics' would be settled in their place.

The missionaries carried out their usual work, which provides us with the few snippets of information we have. At the end of the 11th century, the bishop of Merseburg ordered the cutting down of a sacred grove. In 1123, a Spanish missionary had to be rescued by pagan priests when locals were outraged at his attempt to destroy a pagan image at Wolin, on the Polish Baltic coast. Over a hundred years later, Bishop Gerold of Lübeck destroyed a sacred oaken grove and statues dedicated to the deity Prove, god of justice. Contemporary evidence of the nature of Slavic religion in the region is otherwise sparse. Archaeology shows that, as in England and elsewhere, prehistoric burial mounds and megaliths continued to hold religious significance. A Slavic burial was inserted into a Bronze Age barrow at Waren, and a survey of megaliths in the Mecklenburg-Vorpommern region found that 31% contained Slavic-era items, including a 9th-century Arabic coin.

Polabian Slavs, as well as other Baltic peoples, apparently paid tribute at the major sanctuary to the god Sventovit on the German Baltic island of Rügen. Here, at Arkona, according to the 12th-century Danish historian Saxo Grammaticus, there was a quadrangular wooden temple to Sventovit ministered by pagan priests. Excavations in the 1920s by the renowned German archaeologist Carl Schuchhard found evidence, albeit hardly conclusive, that seemed to match Saxo's description. As to the statue of Sventovit:

> A huge idol stood in the temple, surpassing in its size any human stature, amazing with its four heads and necks; of them two seemed to look from his chest and two from his back ... In his right hand he carried a horn adorned with various metals. The priest, expert in the rites, used to fill this with wine once a year, to judge from the actual state of the liquid the bountifulness of the coming year. His left hand was depicted holding a bow, with his arm drawn in to his side.

Saxo also mentions other wooden idols of multi-headed gods worshipped at sites on the island. He tells of the oaken seven-headed Rugievit at Karentia, and the statue of Porevit with five heads. Further east, the Pomeranian Slavs in what is now Poland were said to have large sanctuaries to a triple-headed god, Triglav, who, like Svantovit, was associated with horse-riding. According to 12th-century chronicles, the internal walls of a temple to Triglav at Stettin (Szczecin) were covered with sculptures and paintings. One-tenth of all battle spoils were consecrated to the god, so the temples were also filled with riches such as golden bowls and knives, and horn goblets decorated with precious stones.

Once again, of course, all these accounts are from the triumphant Christian chroniclers. The descriptions of the Triglav temples come from hagiographies of Bishop Otto of Bamburg (1062–1139). They record that at Stettin he declined to seize the temple treasures, and only kept the head of the wooden idol of Triglav, which he sent to Rome as proof of his good works. Another source of information on the temple of Sventovit, the *Chronica Slavorum*, by the 12th-century Saxon priest Helmold of Bosau, records its destruction in 1168 by the invading Danish King Valdemar. He ordered that the idol be dragged before his soldiers and the local Slavs before being chopped up and burned.

It has been argued that such accounts are thoroughly untrustworthy as sources, with the descriptions of temples and idols amongst the western Slavs being based more on medieval ecclesiastical understanding of classical paganism and Hebraic idolatry than on informed knowledge of religious worship in the region. Linguistic studies, for instance, suggest that the earliest Slavic languages did not recognize the concepts of priests, temples, and idols. Then again, the archaeology does provide limited supporting evidence for the temple structures reported by the hagiographers and chroniclers. Excavations at Wroclaw, a town on the River Oder, and at Wolin revealed evidence of planked ritual buildings containing fragments of silken and golden fabrics. Tree-ring dating suggests that the 'temple' building at Wroclaw was constructed in 1032 or 1033, and recent Polish studies conclude that the western Slavs only began temple building in the 10th century, perhaps in response to Christian influences, which would explain the linguistic evidence mentioned earlier.

Scandinavian religion

Considering how well known Thor and Odin are in modern popular culture, it may seem surprising that contemporary sources on pre-Christian Scandinavian religion are actually few and far between. We do not have the equivalents of Tacitus's *Germania* or Caesar's *Gallic Wars*. The early Christian missionaries evidently came away from their brief sojourns in Scandinavia with little information about the beliefs and practices of the people there. The reason why we think we know so much about Viking paganism is because of the wonderful literary resources that are the sagas, which tell of the voyages and dynastic histories of pagan and Christian Vikings, and the poetic mythological eddas. They were written mostly by Icelandic authors between the 12th and 14th centuries, long after Norwegian settlers had first colonized the island in the 9th century, and nearly two centuries after most of the Viking world had adopted Christianity. While the authors of most of the sagas and eddas no doubt drew upon oral stories recording events stretching back into pre-Christian times, some of their work is clearly the product of poetic imagination. Either way, it cannot be taken for granted that they accurately reflect pre-Christian Scandinavian religions.

So, as to how the gods were actually worshipped, which ones, and where, we have only a sketchy idea. Place-name studies, while fraught with interpretive problems, provide important indications. There are many place names in Scandinavia suggesting pre-Christian religious worship. Some names refer to the gods, and their geographical pattern is obviously significant. Thor is found throughout Scandinavia, while Odin is found frequently enough in Swedish and Danish names but is rare in Norway and Iceland. The god Ull is common in Sweden but not Denmark, and likewise the fertility goddess Freyja is relatively uncommon in Denmark compared to Sweden. Then there are place names that refer to locations of religious significance. The element *lund* means a sacred grove in some contexts but not necessarily always. *Vi* could denote an ancient communal meeting place at which ritual activity took place, while *stallr* might refer to a sacrificial altar, and *hǫrgr* a stone pile supporting an idol. There is an eddic poem in which Freyja says of a great warrior:

> He raised a *hǫrgr* for me
> Piled with stones;
> Now all that rock
> Has turned to glass
> He reddened it anew
> With blood of oxen.

Runic inscriptions also provide some linguistic evidence. The runic alphabet seems to have been first used amongst Germanic and Scandinavian peoples some time in the 2nd century AD. Various versions then developed over the next thousand years. The evidence they provide for pre-Christian religious practices is fragmentary, though. There are examples of Viking-age runes that were clearly pagan, such as invocations to Thor – 'May Thor bless' – and runes were inscribed on stones associated with pagan-era burials. But most of the surviving rune stones date to the early years of Christianity – indeed, they are an important guide to its spread. Before the establishment of churches and churchyards, carved rune-stone crosses marked the presence of the new faith in the landscape and provided a means for the wealthy to continue to memorialize their dead in a traditional form. Scholars used to think that plain rune stones, without crosses or other Christian symbols, were pagan in inspiration, though most are now thought to be Christian too. An interpretive problem concerns the presence of what appear to be pre-Christian symbols and motifs, such as Thor's hammer, on Christian rune stones. Yet some of the imagery can be interpreted in several ways. A scene on one Swedish stone has been explained as depicting the story of Thor catching the world-serpent using the head of an ox as bait, while it has also been interpreted as God using Christ as bait in order to lure Leviathan. Take your pick.

Today runes are commonly associated with pagan magic, but most surviving examples of such usage date to the Christian era. Several of the hundreds of wooden rune sticks found during excavations in Bergen, Norway, which date to between the 12th and 15th century, clearly have magical purposes. One of them begins:

> I cut cure-runes;
> once against the elves,
> twice against the trolls,
> thrice against the ogres.

A few written charms and spells from this period, and earlier, also refer to pagan gods. The extent to which the use of runes in magic was a continuation of a pre-Christian practice is difficult to assess, though. While in medieval Scandinavia runes came to be interpreted by the clergy as the remnants of paganism and so diabolic, it is possible that the magical quality of runes came to the fore in popular practice only once Christianity was well established and the Latin alphabet was adopted.

We saw earlier the problems surrounding the issue of pagan temples in west Slavic culture, and similar issues arise with regard to Viking Scandinavia. The ritual site at Uppsala, Sweden, is well known, but its fame derives solely from the sensational account of the 11th-century German clergyman Adam of Bremen. He reported that rituals there centred on a sacred grove where idols of Thor, Odin, and Freyja were venerated. Every nine years a great sacrificial festival would take place.

> Nine heads are offered from every kind of living creature of the male sex, and the custom is to appease the gods with their blood. But the decapitated bodies are hung in a grove near the temple. The grove was so sacred for pagans that they held each of the trees as divine because of the victims' death. Dogs were hung with horses and men, and a Christian told me that he had seen as many as seventy-two corpses hanging in rows.

There is no reason to trust Adam's account, which, like so many of the period, was not based on first-hand experience. Until recently, excavations beneath the church at Mære, Trondheim, Norway, provided the only substantive evidence for a possible ritual structure. Several small pieces of gold foil that were found have been interpreted as votive offerings.

New excavations are revealing a more complex picture. A Viking-age building at Borg, Sweden, had an outdoor paved area on which several rings were found along with a large quantity of animal bones. The most spectacular finds are from another Swedish site, Uppåkra, where numerous valuable objects, including 111 gold-foil plaques, were found associated with a large building that was the centre for ritual activity for a surprisingly long period – from the 2nd to the 10th centuries. The building was undoubtedly deliberately sited close to several Bronze Age burial mounds. Over 300 weapons and iron implements were deposited in the building, and they exhibit the familiar practice of having been rendered unfit for warfare before placement. Most of these finds date to the 6th and 7th centuries, and so just before what scholars understand as the Viking era (8th to 11th centuries). While the evidence shows that the site retained its ritual significance into the 10th century, it would be a stretch to describe it as a 'Viking temple'.

Religious worship amongst Viking-era pagan Scandinavians was likely to have been highly localized. It was certainly based on animal sacrifices, or *blót*. These blood offerings were thought to strengthen the gods and so make them better predisposed to helping humankind. In the eddas and sagas, horses, cattle, and pigs are the animals most often described as being sacrificed during great indoor banquets that accompanied community assemblies. At Hofstir in Iceland, the excavation in 1908 of an assembly of cattle skulls at a large 10th-century hall suggested to the archaeologists that they had found an example of a temple site that matched the literary descriptions, such as the account in the Eyrbyggja Saga of pagan temples served by a priestly hierarchy and funded by the collection of a temple tax. Recent excavations, and re-interpretation of the site from a more sceptical position regarding the literary sources, suggest that the building, and the feasting that took place in it, was more political than religious. No temple then, but ritual activity was clearly taking place.

Communal pagan worship was probably more generally conducted in open-air sacred spots – mountains, springs, bogs, lakes, burial mounds, and groves. Good evidence for this comes from a 10th-century site at Frösö ('Island of Freyja') in Sweden. A tree stump was excavated underneath a church on the island, around which were found a large number of bones from domesticated and wild animals, including bears, with skulls particularly evident. The tree around which this ritual activity occurred may have represented Yggdrasil, the world tree associated with Odin in Norse mythology. The archaeology suggests the animals were hung from the tree. The ultimate *blót*, human sacrifice, is described in the sagas, but the same issues that were raised in Chapter 2 regarding the reality of the practice apply to the Viking era too.

Viking colonizers: early adopters

The king of Denmark Harald Bluetooth converted around AD 965, marking Christianity's first firm foothold in Scandinavia. In Norway, Kings Olaf I and Olaf II, who reigned between 995 and 1030, enforced the conversion of their peoples and brought in English missionaries to spread the word. Christianity was formally adopted in Iceland in AD 1000. The conversion process was not without hiccups in Denmark and Norway, but it took much longer for the Church to gain influence over Sweden. Missionary activity had occurred there as far back as the 9th century, and King Olaf Skötkonung was baptized by an English missionary in AD 1008, but political as much as religious conflict hampered the uptake of the new faith and the abandonment of the old. It was only in the early 12th century that Christianity was fully established. In 1164, the first archbishop of Sweden was consecrated at Uppsala. It is remarkable, in contrast, how swiftly the pagan Vikings who so successfully set off on their colonial conquests became Christians, at least nominally, soon after settling abroad.

'Never before has such terror appeared in Britain as we have now suffered from a pagan race', wrote Alcuin of York in 793. He was talking, of course, about the Viking raids that had been taking place along the North Sea coast during the late 8th century. From around the 850s, the Danish raiding parties began to overwinter, and then in 865 a large force landed in East Anglia under the leadership of Halfdan and Ivar the Boneless. Intent on conquest, they took over the kingdom of Northumbria and Ivar installed himself as King at York. Within a couple of decades, the Danelaw, the area of Viking influence, stretched across East Anglia, the Midlands, and the North East. Further small-scale settlement took place on the other side of the country, with Vikings from Ireland settling down in the Wirral, parts of Cumbria, and Lancashire. Ivar's successor Guthrum, well known for his unsuccessful struggle against Alfred of Wessex, converted to Christianity in 878 and received the Anglo-Saxon name of Æthelstan. It was an overtly political act to seal a treaty with Wessex.

When the Vikings conquered parts of Britain, there was no pagan crusade or rolling back of Christianity. The old view that the raids on churches and monasteries were religiously inspired, a pagan challenge to Christendom, is no longer accepted. The Vikings were primarily after loot. Once settled in a country in which Christianity and the Church were well established, the Vikings quickly gave up overt signs of their previous forms of worship. Political alignments and intermarriage with the native population further expedited the process of Christianization.

Good archaeological evidence for Viking pagan worship in England is rare and limited largely to sites dating to the military conquest. One example is the cremation cemetery at Heath Wood, Ingleby, Derbyshire, consisting of sixty or so mounds containing cremations of humans and animals. It is likely to have been constructed by an overwintering Viking force in 873–4. Viking army burials at the minster of nearby Repton include a warrior with his sword, boar's tusk amulet, and Thor's hammer pendant. Evidence that Viking settlers maintained pagan traditions in the longer term is less clear-cut. The inclusion of grave goods in otherwise Christian burial contexts has been interpreted as an expression of Scandinavian paganism, though, as was explained in the last chapter, doubt has been cast on the use of burial goods as a guide to the religious beliefs of those interred. It is certainly the case, however, that religious sculptures and stone crosses found in and around churches in northern England contain motifs from Nordic religion such as runes and mythological figures. The extent to which they represent a syncretic fusion of the two religions is debatable. It has been argued that the use of such symbols and motifs was cultural rather than specifically religious in inspiration.

The quality of evidence for Scotland, which saw considerable settlement in the Northern Isles of Orkney and Shetland and along the western coastline, is similar. In the Northern Isles, which were Christianized around 995 according to traditional chronology, there are a few rune stones but mostly of 12th century date, and so are highly unlikely to have been the work of pagan Vikings. There are quite a few graves that are probably pagan, one sign being flexed burial, but few date to beyond the mid-10th century. Otherwise, there are only a few examples of cremation, one of the clearest signs of pre-Christian Scandinavian religion. Further round the coast, excavations on the Isle of Man have revealed evidence for Viking pagan burial practices in the 10th century, most notably the Chapel Hill ship burial which was deliberately cut through an earlier Christian cemetery. Was it an aggressive act reasserting pagan worship on the island? Or was it a mark of respect – recognition of a sacred Christian site?

The 'North men', mostly Danish Vikings, had raided the French coast since the early 9th century. In 841, Asgeir pillaged and burned down the town of Rouen. A Viking fleet even sailed up the Seine and attacked Paris in 885. By around AD 900, under the leadership of Hrolfe, or Rollo as he was called in French chronicles, the Vikings were firmly settled along the northern coast between Picardy and Brittany and along the banks of the lower Seine. After defeating Rollo's forces in 911, the Frankish King Charles the Simple (879–929) thought it expedient not to wage further war and granted Rollo control over the region of what we now know as Normandy, the 'Kingdom of the Northmen'. As part of the deal, Rollo accepted the Christian faith and was baptized as 'Robert'. As was the usual state of affairs, once the ruler converted so too his people were forced to do so. His son William Longsword, a devout Christian, sealed relations by marrying a Frankish princess.

There is practically no evidence for the reception of Christianization amongst the Viking settlers. The situation must have been complicated, since new pagan settlers from the North kept arriving in Normandy up until the 930s. Evidence that the exercise was not straightforward comes from a letter to the archbishop of Rouen, dating to between 914 and 922, which refers to advice on evangelizing the settlers, and suggests a possible relapse into pagan practices. Suspicions about the Normans circulated. What sounds like a scurrilous rumour regarding Rollo was reported by Adhemar of Chabannes a century after his death. Adhemar relates that at the end of his life Rollo hedged his bets by distributing huge amounts of gold to the Church while at the same time sacrificing captives to his old Nordic gods.

The Norwegian Vikings, or *Gaill* (foreigners) as they were frequently referred to in Irish chronicles, first began raiding the Irish coast in the years around 800, with attacks increasing in the 830s. They came looking for slaves as well as monastic riches. In the early 1840s, they began to overwinter, founding bases for further raids. One of these was the foundation for Dublin. Danes would soon begin to challenge the Norwegians for power in the land. While conflict took place because of the Viking presence in Ireland, there was no long-lasting bloody war between the Irish and the invaders. Alliances were forged, and intermarriage took place. The Irish aristocracy benefited from the international trade network of the Vikings, and they knew it.

The Vikings obviously arrived as pagans in a country that had fully adopted Christianity two centuries earlier, and in which monasteries and an organized Church were well established. As to the pre-Christian religion of Ireland, we once again rely heavily on myths and stories, such as the 'Ulster Cycle', written down by medieval monks. They relate legendary events of dynastic feuding, epic cattle raids, and druidic magicians supposed to have occurred around the time of Christ. The archaeological evidence certainly attests to the fact that the pre-Christian Irish shared similar ritual activities to Iron Age societies elsewhere, but the extent to which they shared a pan-European 'Celtic' or druidic religion is a matter of speculation and wishful thinking rather than historical certainty.

As in France and England, the Vikings would come to adopt the religion of their new Irish homeland, but scholars disagree significantly about when and how. Dates suggested for the conversion of the Dublin Vikings range from the mid-9th century to the early 11th century. The meagre archaeological and place-name evidence does not help much, so we are reliant on the literary archive. The term *geinti* (gentile) is frequently applied to the Vikings until 877, but then drops out of usage. It reappears again in various documents from the early 10th century. What does this signify? It could mean that the Viking settlers had generally converted by the 880s, and then a new wave of visitors from pagan Scandinavia pitched up several decades later. Assessing the religious persuasion of the Irish Vikings is clearly a very inexact science, and as a trading post it is likely that the Scandinavian presence in Ireland was a mix of Christian and pagan until the 11th century.

Baltic stronghold

Other than the Saami herder communities of the far north of Scandinavia, the last non-Christian societies in Europe were in the Baltic lands of Lithuania, Estonia, and Latvia. One reason it took Christianity so long to reach the peoples who lived in the region – the Livs, Prussians, Letts, Ests, Zemgalians, Selonians, and others – was simply their distance from Rome and Byzantium, and from the missionary training grounds of Britain and Ireland. That is not to say that this region of marshes and forests was immune from Christian influence. Danish and German traders, who would later form the Hanseatic League, provided a vehicle for missionary activity. A bishopric had been instituted in Livonian territory in 1191. But the real challenge came with the growing power and aggression of the Knights of the Sword of Livonia and the Teutonic Knights of Prussia. It was their brutal conquest that forced Christianity upon Estonia in 1208–27.

The Lithuanians were the last to hold out, but the picture is far from one of a crude pagan versus Christian struggle. For one, the kingdom was influenced not only by Roman Catholicism but also by the Byzantine Orthodox Church, which had a strong foothold in the eastern Slavic territories, such as Kievan Rus, captured by the Lithuanians. The history of religion in the country in the 13th and 14th centuries is, in fact, one of toleration. The pagan Lithuanian aristocracy, notably the powerful Gediminas (d. 1341), allowed the presence of Orthodox and Catholic churches, while the converted kings, such as Mindaugas (1253–63), did not impose their new faith on their subjects. Indeed, the Roman Catholic Mindaugas, if the accounts are to be believed, continued to conduct sacrifices. As a papal legate put it, writing in 1312, Mindaugas 'was a Christian and kept clergy but he still maintained his earlier errors'.

4. Pagan Bulgars massacring Christians. Medieval depiction of the Battle of Pliska, which took place in 811. The Bulgars, led by Khan Krum, inflicted a terrible defeat on the Byzantine army

Lithuania's official Christian status began with the conversion of King Jogaila in 1386. Yet the Lithuanians continued to attract a reputation for paganism around Europe well into the 15th century. Numerous accusations were levelled at the successful military leader Vytautas, who was ruler of the Grand Duchy of Lithuania between 1392 and 1430. He had ordered the building of churches and promoted the faith, yet he was accused of being a polytheist, and his people of being heathens, or 'saracens' to equate them with the Islamic occupants of the Holy Land. His military initiatives were denounced as springing from anti-Christian motives. These accusations were very much politically inspired, scare tactics used by the Teutonic Knights to maintain papal backing for lucrative crusades against the Lithuanians. In 1415, Vytautas tried to put an end to the accusations by sending a delegation of Samogitians (from north-western Lithuania) to a papal Council in order to reaffirm their Catholicism, and request the creation of a bishopric in Samogitia. Their request was granted, dealing a terminal political blow to the power of the Teutonic Knights.

There are few contemporary sources about the nature of the religious beliefs and practices of the Baltic peoples, and a good deal of (problematic) reconstruction has taken place using folklore

5. Olaus Magnus, *Historia de Gentibus Septentrionalibus* (1555). Idolatrous Lithuanians praying before two altars, one with a fire and the other a serpent

collected in the 19th and 20th centuries. Three gods have been identified as particularly important, the thunder god Perkūnas (equated with Perun), the warrior god Andojas, and the smith god Teliavel/Kalevelis. As elsewhere in northern Europe, the concepts of temples and priesthoods can be considered as late and brief developments, if they existed at all. The account of a great Baltic temple or sacred place at Romuva, presided over by a 'pagan pope', written by the Teutonic chronicler Peter von Duisburg around 1326, is generally considered to be a figment of hearsay and imagination.

Contemporary reports suggest that worship was centred on woodland groves, or *alkos*, where sacrifices were burned. A witness at the coronation of Mindaugas in 1253 noted that his peoples worshipped at sacred trees. He also reported that 'they burned their dead with their horses and weapons and better apparel because they believe they may use these and the other things they burn in the next world'. Documents of the Teutonic Order refer to sacred groves as landmarks in the countryside, and in the late 16th century Jesuit missionaries, who were primarily concerned with combating Protestantism and Orthodox religion in the region, reported that groves still held significance to the common people. In Estonia, ethnographic data might suggest that as well as groves, holy stones, mostly natural granite boulders, were the locations of religious offerings. Some 400 or so have been identified, with a small number having prehistoric cup marks. There is no evidence, though, linking the medieval and more recent veneration of such stones with prehistoric patterns of worship. Furthermore, the ethnographic data mostly refers to their use in healing rituals which need not be related to religious worship.

Chapter 4
Pagans across the oceans

As we have seen, the Church had been shaped by and defined itself in relation to the other religions it encountered in Europe and the Mediterranean world. The age of exploration across the oceans from the late 15th century onwards brought Christians into contact with entirely new peoples and new religions. They encountered tribes and civilizations unknown to the Greeks and Romans, and which had no place in Old Testament history. They were a great puzzle. How to make sense of their existence and their belief systems? At first, the old vocabulary pertaining to the 'other' sufficed. The populations of the Americas, Africa, and Asia were heathens, barbarians, savages, gentiles, pagans.

It slowly dawned, though, that these overseas pagans far outnumbered Christians in the world. This was a state of affairs that could not be tolerated, and so a new front opened up for the Church's army of missionaries.

Early encounters

Confronted by Europeans for the first time, with their strange dress, armaments, and ships, some of the indigenous peoples of the Americas concluded that these peculiar beings were deities to be worshipped and supplicated. When, in 1519, Magellan landed at what is now Rio de Janeiro, the local Guaraní apparently thought the sailors were rain-bringing gods. In other words, the Europeans became, albeit briefly, part of the cosmologies of these societies. Their sudden and sensational appearance fitted the notion, widespread in many religions (including Christianity of course), of the return of divine beings that herald a new age of renewal. The Catholic invaders exploited this interpretation, with Christians playing 'pagan' gods when it suited their aims. When Hernando de Soto (d. 1542) encountered the indigenous inhabitants around the banks of the Mississippi in 1541, he communicated to them that he was the child of their sun god and demanded their worship. One of the downfalls of the Aztecs was that their ruler Moctezuma feared the conquistador Hernán Cortés was the god Quetzalcoatl, a belief that Cortés was happy to exploit. Francis Drake (d. 1596), on the other hand, declined to play pagan god when he landed on the pacific American coast, somewhere north of San Francisco, in 1579. He soon encountered the local Miwok tribe who prostrated themselves before him and offered gifts. Drake ordered the ship's chaplain to read from the Bible while Drake indicated to the Miwok that he was no deity by pointing away from himself and towards the sky.

These various early accounts were written by the Europeans, of course, and not by the indigenous people. We cannot be certain that the chroniclers' interpretations of these encounters are correct. Still, folk traditions recorded from some Native Americans several generations after these first encounters show that the European ships were believed to be the dwelling places of powerful spirits who needed to be supplicated and appeased. Furthermore, there are also the comparative examples of the cargo cults that arose on some of the islands in the south-western Pacific following the arrival of Europeans and their material wealth in the 19th and 20th centuries. The ascription of divine virtues to pale-faced 'big men' even led to the British Prince Philip being worshipped by people on the island of Tanna.

Missionaries

Missionary activity was a fundamental part of European trade and colonization. While the conquest of the Americas by the Spanish and Portuguese was driven by the search for wealth, it was also an opportunity for the Roman Catholic Church to recruit large numbers of new souls to compensate for losses in Europe following the Protestant Reformation. They encountered a huge diversity of peoples from Aztec and Inca urban societies to small hunter-gatherer tribes deep in the rain forests. The forms of religious belief expressed were diverse and localized. What struck the Europeans most, though, were the large pantheon of deities that were worshipped, the elaborate ritual calendars, and the practice of sacrifice amongst the Incas and Aztecs: all traits characteristic of 'Old World' paganism, and abhorrent to the Christian conquerors.

There are numerous examples of the disregard and brutality with which conquistadors and missionaries treated native populations. Writing in the mid-16th century, the Spanish Franciscan friar Pedro Aguado described the slow progress of conversion in Colombia partly because the natives lived 'against the law of nature, more like wild beasts than human beings'. Many were forcibly baptized and enslaved. There were compassionate voices too, particularly those of priests of the Society of Jesus. The Jesuits were founded by Ignatius Loyola in 1540 with the sole aim of spreading Catholicism across the known world. Their defining strategy when attempting to convert indigenous peoples was to live amongst them, learn their culture and language. They operated like anthropologists, though their aim was primarily to understand in order to identify aspects of native religious, social, and moral life that were similar to or reconcilable with Catholicism, and those elements that were anathema. A letter written by the Jesuit José de Anchieta during his stay in Brazil in 1554 highlights this well.

He had nothing positive to say about one group of 'Indians' amongst whom he had worked:

> all of them eat human flesh, go about nude ... they are not subject to any king or leader ... Living without law or government, it follows they can't live in peace and harmony amongst themselves ... Added to this is the fact that, [since they] contract marriage with their own relatives, even [first] cousins, it is difficult if we want to baptise [a man], to find a woman who, because of blood kinship, can be taken as [a legitimate] wife.

In contrast, he wrote that the Ibirajaras tribe were superior to all the others

> in the use of reason and in their intelligence and the gentleness of [their] customs. All of them obey one chief, they have a great horror of eating human flesh, they are satisfied with only one wife, and they carefully protect their virgin daughters ... Only one thing appears to be worthy of rebuke among them, [which] is that, they sometimes kill captives in war and keep their heads as trophies.

So some pagans were considered closer to possible salvation than others, by dint of their display of what were considered Christian qualities. Francis Drake wrote of the Miwok that they were 'of a tractable, free, and loving nature, without guile or treachery'. The Dominican friar Alonso de Espinosa, writing around 1590, described the Guanches of Tenerife as 'uncontaminated Gentiles' who were 'without any law, nor ceremonies, nor gods like other nations'. Untouched by contact with Islam, he considered them one step away from the Christian faith rather than opposed or a threat to it. His sympathies did not extend to the population of the neighbouring island of Gran Canaria, though.

Although the Catholic Church had a considerable head start, and a monopoly over Central and South America, the Protestant churches proved equally zealous in their missionary activity. In

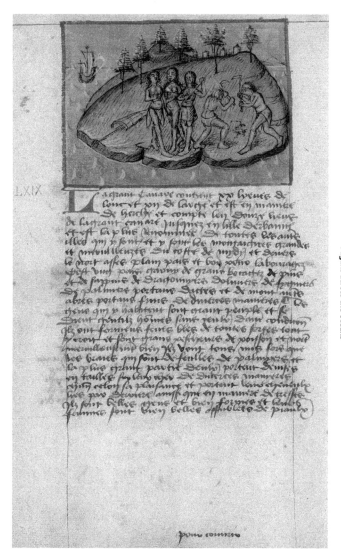

6. Pagan natives of the island of 'Enfer' (Hell), the French description of Tenerife, from *Le Canarien*, a French chronicle of an expedition to the Canary Islands in 1402

7. Olaus Magnus, *Historia de Gentibus Septentrionalibus* (1555). Magnus's *History of the Northern People* depicts the idolatrous animistic worship of the peoples of the Arctic region

1722, the Norwegian Lutheran missionary Hans Egede (1686–1758) and a small band of like-minded souls, established the first European settlement in Greenland since the Vikings arrived there in the late 10th century. Egede's mission, on behalf of the Danish king, was to convert the descendants of the Viking Greenlanders who, untouched by the Reformation, would have remained Catholic or perhaps had reverted to paganism. Much to their disappointment, they found the old colony had long since disappeared. As we now know from archaeological work, after 500 years' existence the settlement had become extinct in the 16th century as the agricultural economy that sustained the community suffered a mini 'ice age'. Egede turned his attention to converting the native Inuit population instead. He described them as 'naturally very stupid and indolent', and opined that their 'ignorance of a Creator would make one believe they were Atheists'. But as he believed they had 'some notion of the immortality of souls', he thought there was some spiritual soil in which to plant the seeds of Christianity.

As for the Swedish and Danish kingdoms (the latter included Norway), there were pagans much closer to home who also required attention. The religious beliefs of the Saami, whose

8. Example of a Saami ritual drum used for divination and in the performance of other magic rituals

territory stretched across Arctic Scandinavia, had been brought to wide attention in the mid-16th century by an account of them published in a book entitled *The History of the Northern People* (1555). Its author, Olaus Magnus, was the last Catholic bishop in Sweden before the country became Lutheran. It was not until the late 17th century, though, that a mix of ethnographic curiosity and missionary zeal led to a concerted attempt both to understand and suppress Saami religion, and what was described as their 'idolatry', 'sorcery', and 'superstition'. In 1685, a Swedish Royal Edict instituted a systematic attempt to eradicate the drums used by Saami shamans. Norwegian missionaries were also particularly active in the early 18th century seeking out and destroying the sacred sites of the Saami.

Further east, in Russia, the Mari, a nomadic people related to the Saami, were targeted for conversion by the Russian Orthodox Church and the state as part of the creation of imperial Russia from the 16th century onwards. The Maris believed in a supreme God (Kugu Jumo), but on a day-to-day basis venerated a variety of nature spirits, to whom they performed sacrifices of domestic animals and produce in sacred groves in order to protect family and community. There were brutal campaigns of conversion against such 'pagans' (*iazychniki*) under Ivan the Terrible (1530–84) and Peter the Great (1672–1725), but the main period of systematic conversion of the Mari was during the 18th century, when the vast majority were recorded as being Christian converts. In the process, they gave up considerable religious autonomy for the legal benefits of becoming baptized Russians.

Bringing civilization?

A common, though not always explicit, conviction amongst missionaries and their supporters was that their task was not solely a matter of baptizing but also about instigating the civilization process amongst pagans. Never mind that the greatest civilizations in the ancient world, whose intellectual and creative achievements continued to have a profound influence on the forging of modern society, were pagan. Christianity brought industry, enlightenment, and progress, while paganism was synonymous with backwardness. The stereotypical pagan was fatalistic, indolent, superstitious, puerile, and born to be subjugated. Being a Christian was not only a matter of accepting the faith but of adopting European cultural and social values. Converts were expected to wear European clothing, live settled lives, till the soil, mix only with other Christians, and live in square or rectangular rather than round dwellings.

This agenda was laid uncomfortably bare in early 19th-century North America, where the terms 'Christian Party' and 'Pagan Party' were used to describe the political and social divisions missionary activity caused amongst Native Americans. The Native American chief most associated with the so-called 'Pagan Party' was the famed orator Sagoyewatha, or Red Jacket, of the Seneca Nation. Red Jacket (d. 1830) campaigned for the protection of Seneca lands from the machinations of the land-grabbing Ogden Land Company, and for the protection of Seneca traditions and lifestyle from the work of missionaries. Once asked why he opposed missionaries, he replied:

> Because they do us no good. If they are not useful to the white people, why do they send them among the Indians...We cannot read their book; they tell us different stories about what it contains, and we believe they make the book talk to suit themselves.

In missionary publications of the 1820s, those European Americans who expressed support for Red Jacket's stance were labelled 'white pagans'. Several decades later, there were signs of more sensitivity about the missionaries' cultural assumptions, particularly as the missions were becoming seen as branches of the state. In 1856, the American Board of Commissioners for Foreign Missions stated:

Missions are instituted for the spread of scriptural self-propagating Christianity. This is their only aim. Civilization as an end, they never attempt; still they are the most successful of all civilizing agencies ... a rapid change in the intellectual and social life is a sure growth therefrom.

Eastern religions

When missionaries turned to the East, they found great empires, sophisticated literary cultures, and organized religions with ancient founding texts. The Jesuit missionary Matteo Ricci (1552–1610) established the first Christian station on mainland China in 1583, during the reign of the Ming dynasty. Ricci found Confucianism to be the most politically influential belief system, while the common people generally followed Buddhism and Taoism. Ricci's study of Confucian texts led him to the conclusion that its roots lay in monotheism. This, and the antiquity of the Chinese language, suggested that Christian doctrines were hidden in the ancient texts. The Chinese were not like the pagans his fellow Jesuits reported having encountered in the Americas. The Franciscans and Dominicans who first arrived in China in the 1630s were not so sympathetic to the religious cultures of the Chinese, however, or Ricci's interpretation of the Christian themes in Confucianism. Chinese ancestor worship, and associated ritual practices involving the burning of incense in front of tablets bearing the names of the dead, were denounced as idolatry. The Jesuits were accused of deliberately omitting details of such pagan practices from the various sympathetic books and reports they had produced on Chinese religion, which had attracted considerable European intellectual interest. The Jesuits argued in response that such rites were secular expressions of respect.

In 1724, the Chinese Imperial government banned Catholicism and Protestantism along with other 'perverse sects and sinister doctrines'. Catholic and Protestant missionaries nevertheless continued to pursue their work in areas beyond government control. But European knowledge of Chinese religion remained heavily reliant on the earlier published work of the Jesuits. We can still see their influence in the early 19th century. The clergyman and chronicler of world religions, the Reverend Robert Adam, related the view that Confucius was 'the noblest and most divine philosopher of the pagan world', who remained untainted by the introduction of the 'monstrous idols that, in after ages, disgraced the temples of China'.

The tendency at this time was still to define 'religion' as the big three monotheistic theologies of the Near East – Christianity, Judaism, and Islam – with all the rest lumped together as 'modern paganism'. This was certainly the system adopted in the Reverend Adam's hefty two-volume *The Religious World Displayed* (1823), which was a survey of global religion as known in the West at that time. Adam's contemporary, the American compiler of religious creeds John Hayward, defined paganism in the broadest of terms as 'applied to Heathen Idolaters, who worship false gods, and are not acquainted either with the doctrines of the Old Testament or the Christian dispensation'. On this basis, he estimated that pagans made up more than half the population of the globe.

According to Adam, Confucianism as a belief system was 'certainly not so gross and unnatural as that of the Hindoos'. When Roman Catholic missionaries began to push inland from Portuguese coastal bases in India during the 16th century, they found a number of small Christian communities already long established by missionaries who had travelled to India overland during the medieval period. Relations between the native churches and the new Roman Catholic missionaries were far from harmonious, and the initial successes of the Jesuits in China were not matched in India. The fact that by 1700 much of the Indian subcontinent was under the rule of the Islamic Mughal Empire obviously severely restricted Christian European influence. Furthermore, until the early 19th century, the British East India Company, whose control

9. Title page from an 18th-century edition of an account of the East Indies by the Dutch minister Philip Baldæus, first published in 1671. Baldæus describes the 'pagan' temples and beliefs he encountered in Ceylon (Sri Lanka) and the southern coast of India

over large parts of India had expanded over the previous century, had banned missionary access to areas under its influence, fearing that their activity would antagonize the native population and upset trade relations. The ban was lifted in 1813, and missionary activity increased hugely in a vain attempt to Christianize the 'benighted Hindoo'. Publications and reports commonly referred to 'Hindoo pagans' and the 'absurdities of Hindoo paganism'. Hopes for successful mass conversion were clearly high, for in 1815 the London Missionary Society reported confidently that 'many of the detestable practices of Hindoo pagans are retiring before the light of the Gospel'.

The two key practices that made Hindoo and pagan interchangeable in Christian eyes were the worship of multiple gods and what one observer, writing in 1831, called the 'horrid rites of paganism' concerning the burning rather than burial of the dead. 'Sacrifice' was a word that also frequently cropped up in accounts of *sati*, the custom of widows being burned on the pyres along with their deceased husbands, which fascinated and horrified British readers long after it was outlawed in 1829. But, as elsewhere, missionaries perceived varying levels of entrenched paganism in Hinduism depending on local cultures. Missionaries in the Jaffna peninsula in Sri Lanka, writing in 1817, reported contentedly that in the district of Columbo the Hindu population was 'less devotedly attached to their idolatrous rites, have feebler prejudices against Christianity... than in almost any other part of the pagan world'.

It was in the myriad islands of the Indonesian and Malaysian archipelagos that missionaries believed they encountered the worst excesses of paganism in the forms of head hunting and cannibalism. As described in the book *Universal History Americanised* (1819), the people on some of the islands 'eat the flesh of their enemies... and drink out of their skulls; and the ornaments of their houses are human skulls and teeth. Such is Paganism, in its natural state.' A couple of decades later, a medical

Punans' Heads taken by Sea Dayaks

10. The shrunken, smoked heads of enemies kept by the Dyaks of Borneo

journal noted that these pagan practices explained 'why travellers are so frequently decapitated in those countries'.

The Dyaks of Borneo received particular attention for their head-hunting activities. Although often considered as a 'tribe', the Dyaks were, and are, actually made up of a variety of different localized ethnic groups who share a similar culture and animistic beliefs. Their practice of head hunting was primarily, but not exclusively, associated with notions regarding the spirit world. To combat evil spirits and the misfortune they caused, the Dyaks believed that the spiritual energy residing in the human head could be harvested to provide protection. The fact that it was recognized as a custom of their ancestors was also sufficient to maintain the practice.

The missionaries were not put off by stories of head hunting and cannibalism, however, and some even seemed to relish the challenge of converting these most 'pagan' of peoples in their eyes.

The spreading influence of Islam across the archipelagos was also a strong motivation. In the 1830s, an American missionary report stated that the Dyaks were 'as promising as any untutored race of pagans, and will probably be found more ready to listen to the gospel than the followers of Confucius, or Mohammed'.

Africa and Islam

During the late 15th and the 16th centuries, Jesuits and friars could be found in the Portuguese trading colonies dotted along the West and North African coasts. Their success at converting the general population was very limited, and most effort went into trying to convert local rulers. Later, the iniquity of the slave trade, and the culpability of religious establishments, hardly reflected well on the superiority of the Christian faith in African eyes. Concerted missionary activity by both Catholic and Protestant organizations only really began from the second half of the 18th century onwards. The first Anglican missionary in Africa was the Reverend Thomas Thompson, who was sent to the Gold Coast on behalf of the Society for the Propagation of the Gospel in 1752. Many 19th-century missionaries saw their work introducing 'civilizing' religion as reparation for the horrors inflicted upon Africans by the slave trade.

Missionary reports from the so-called 'Dark Continent' contained the usual descriptions of supposed barbarism, with a particular emphasis on evidence of human sacrifice. While the human sacrifice of captives was practised to propitiate or communicate with the gods, and was particularly associated with the òrìsà religion of the Yoruba, reports of its practice across the continent were often inflated and incorrect. The spectre of this classic 'pagan' activity being alive and well in Africa helped bolster support for European military subjugation, while some rituals of the dead were misinterpreted. When Europeans came across decomposing corpses in woodland groves in southern Nigeria, they believed them to be sacrificial sites, when in fact the groves were where the Igbo people left the corpses of those in their communities who had died 'bad deaths'.

European colonial attitudes towards indigenous religions in Africa were framed by concern over the competing influence of Islam. There was, in effect, a race to convert 'pagans' as a bulwark against the spread of Islam from North Africa. In the words of an 1819 report by the Wesleyan Methodist Missionary Society, Islam filled 'the hearts of the natives with a hatred of Christians unfelt by them in their purely pagan state'. From a missionary point of view, experience showed it was far easier to convert pagans than Muslims. The 19th-century geographers who mapped out the interior of the continent played their part in this race. A report on the 'state of human society' in northern Central Africa to the Royal Geographical Society in 1860 identified the Mossi tribe, who are today mostly located in Burkina Faso, as ancient 'champions of Paganism against Islamism'. Because of this history and its openness to trade, the author recommended that the Mossi kingdom was a good place to establish missions, 'if the Christian nations wish to put a stop to the progress of Islamism'.

It has been suggested by some scholars that there were certain aspects of Islam that made it more appealing than Christianity to the adherents of indigenous African religions. Most important of all was the Muslim toleration of polygamy, which was a practice antithetical to Christian missionary sensibilities. The Muslim conception of djinns, or spirits, particularly in Islamic folk religion, was also similar to those figures in African religions, as were notions of purity and pollution. Broader political, commercial, colonial, and military issues decided most conversions, though.

Success?

Recent statistics on global religions estimate that 33% of the world's population is defined as Christian, 21% Muslim, and 0.22% Jewish. So from an early 19th-century definition, nearly half the world's ever-expanding population is still 'pagan'. This is, of course, not a definition that the vast majority of people would subscribe to today. The category of 'indigenous religions' reflects a much more narrow contemporary perspective on beliefs that display some of the traits that Christians long associated with paganism. It includes Siberian shamanic cultures, African religions, and the related faiths that developed amongst the African diasporas in the Caribbean and the Americas, and this category constitutes around 6% of the world population, or 400 million people. It is, of course, very difficult to accurately estimate adherents of any religion, either in the past or the present, but what these modern statistics show is that, the Americas apart, the historic European Christian missionary impulse was largely a failure in simplistic terms. I say simplistic because if we return to the concept of syncretism, and look carefully at the historic and contemporary evidence, we find many examples of how aspects of Christianity were absorbed into indigenous religions, and vice versa. The influences are subtle and adaptable.

Consider the Iroquois Nation, whose people were described as the 'Romans of this western world' by the governor of New York DeWitt Clinton (1769–1828) because of their eloquence, organization, agriculturalism, civility, and paganism. One branch of the Nation lived in Ontario where, during the period of French rule (1615–1760), the activities of Roman Catholic missionaries had some success in converting them. Under the subsequent British rule, Dutch and British Protestant missionaries then continued the campaign of conversion. Yet by the 20th century, there were still some 1,000 Iroquois practising their traditional religion on the Grand River Reserve in Ontario. But as an anthropological study of their beliefs and traditions published in 1900 and entitled *On the Paganism of the Civilised Iroquois of Ontario* explained, nearly three centuries of dialogue with Christians had had subtle influences over their religious beliefs and practices, principally the way in which forms of Christian prayer had filtered into the worship of Niyoh the Great Spirit. In the

Christian Iroquois communities, there were also many who 'either attend no place of worship at all or would just as soon put in an appearance at a pagan festival'.

So those converted by force or co-opted by material reward might act like Christians but still think like 'pagans'. A 1763 census of religions in Kazan province, Russia, stated that 95% of the 'pagan' population had registered as converts to Christianity. Yet subsequent ethnographic studies show the people of the region continued with their traditional beliefs or fused them with Christianity, as is evident amongst the aforementioned Mari population today – much to the continued annoyance of the Orthodox Church and secular authorities alike.

It is important to stress that Christian perceptions of a faith chasm between their religion and the indigenous religions of those they wished to convert was not necessarily shared by the latter. Conversion from an indigenous religion to Christianity need not have been a fundamental rejection of an individual's or a community's previous patterns of belief. Furthermore, as numerous studies of conversion in Africa have shown, people did not reject their 'paganism' because Christianity was revealed to be any more coherent or 'true'. Local politics, trade, kin relations, access to medicine, opportunities for education and work have all been shown to be important pragmatic factors for conversion.

This complex story of the negotiation and inter-relationships between Christianity and other religions played out everywhere Christianity gained a foothold overseas. It is particularly apparent in the Caribbean, where a series of new belief systems developed amongst the African slave populations in response to their social, cultural, and environmental circumstances. They are characterized by a combination of polytheism and monotheism, animistic concepts, ancestor worship, and mediation between the human and spirit worlds.

The religions of the West African homelands of the former slaves are the basis for such traditions as Orisha in Cuba, Haitian Vodou, and Obeah in the former British Caribbean colonies. Elements of the Christian tradition, and Catholicism in particular, have also been adopted. The followers of Orisha have incorporated the saints into their pantheon of African orishas, or personified nature deities. Each orisha has its corresponding saint identified as possessing similar attributes and powers. So the universal mother Yemayá is equated with the patron saint of the bay of Havana, La Virgen de Regla. Some see this fusion of faiths in the Caribbean as another example of syncretism, but the term 'creolization' is also used to better reflect the dynamism of these traditions, and the empowering processes of adoption and transformation of certain aspects of Christianity. To describe them as pagan is certainly not appropriate.

Chapter 5
Embracing the pagan past

As the first missionaries set about their work across the oceans, back in Europe the Renaissance was in full bloom, and at its heart was the intellectual embrace of pagan antiquity, of its philosophical and artistic achievements. But it is important to recognize that the influence of pre-Christian Greco-Roman intellectualism had never been purged entirely from Christian thought. There was, for example, an enduring theological debate concerning the salvation of the 'virtuous pagans', in other words the great philosophers of antiquity who were ignorant of Christ.

According to Christian theology, only the souls of those who had been baptized could be saved. This meant that everyone prior to the coming of Christ had been damned – pagans and the entire cast of the Old Testament alike. But in the early years of the Church, explanations were sought that might circumvent this historical finality. One controversial solution was the 'Harrowing of Hell' – in other words, the notion that during the three days between Christ's burial and Resurrection, he descended into Hell to defeat the Devil and liberate the souls of the righteous damned. This was by no means unanimously endorsed by the early Church Fathers. A related concept, which was developed in the medieval period, was the existence of limbo, a state of existence on the edge of Hell where the souls of unbaptized children and the Old

Testament patriarchs resided. In the early 14th century, the Italian poet Dante (1265–1321) broke with orthodoxy in his *Divine Comedy* by depicting another separate limbo for the virtuous pagan poets and philosophers of Greco-Roman antiquity. There could be found the souls of Virgil, Ovid, Horace, Homer, Aristotle, Socrates, and Plato. Dante died as the stirrings of the period we know as the Renaissance could be detected, and with it the intellectual and artistic harrowing of the virtuous pagans.

Renaissance

The Renaissance was not so much a break with the past as a re-engagement with antiquity. Thanks to the advent of printing in the late 15th century, the writings of the Greco-Roman philosophers, physicians, historians, scientists, and geographers became available to all who could read Latin, and then subsequently reached an even wider readership when they were gradually translated into the vernacular. In the Mediterranean world, the achievements of the Greco-Romans were not only apparent in literature but in the many surviving architectural monuments. Ancient Roman art such as wall paintings, sculptures, and friezes were copied and re-interpreted in novel depictions of pagan and Christian themes. Romanticized portraits of ancient sacrifice were produced. Italian architects such as Palladio took the designs of pagan temple façades and recreated them in numerous Christian churches.

The ancient pagan philosophy of Neoplatonism attracted renewed attention, inspiring the development of new magical mystical traditions. The discovery in the mid-15th century of a manuscript purportedly containing the occult philosophy of Hermes Trismegistus, the personification of the Greek god Hermes and the Egyptian god of wisdom Thoth, provided an exciting new key to the door of universal secret wisdom. Never mind that this *Corpus Hermeticum* was actually created in the age of early Christianity rather than in an earlier era of the world. Renaissance

11. A classical pagan tomb sacrifice (1526) by Benvenuto Garofalo (1481–1559). His inspiration was a woodcut depicting an ancient rite in the romance *Hypnerotomachia Poliphili* (Dream of Poliphilus), which was published in Venice in 1499

magic drew on these and other antique pagan sources of knowledge, but while some practitioners valued the ancient Egyptian and Greco-Roman pantheons as sources of divine inspiration, they were never afforded parity with the Christian God. Renaissance magicians accorded due respect to the religious wisdom of the ancients, but engaged with it only to attain personal knowledge of the miracle of Christian divinity.

The Renaissance politician and philosopher Niccolò Machiavelli (1469–1527), whose cynical views on the exercise of power and Christianity attracted notoriety after his death, has been described by some recent scholars as a 'genuine pagan'. He certainly sympathized with the religions of ancient Rome, and the strength they gave the individual and the state, but ultimately he neither rejected Christianity nor expressed any interest personally in practising other religions. Writing in 1860, the pioneering historian of Renaissance Italy Jacob Burckhardt claimed disparagingly that the brand of humanism that developed in the late 15th century was 'in fact pagan'. But despite all the suspicions circulating at the time, and the obvious interest in pagan antiquity, there is no evidence of European humanists reviving pre-Christian forms of worship. In this sense, Renaissance paganism was a figment of the imagination.

Renaissance intellectuals, nevertheless, had to square their admiration for the classical authors with their Christian faith. How to make pagan classics safe for general Christian consumption? This troubled consciences to varying degrees. The Dominican priest and Florentine politician Girolamo Savonarola (1452–98) was adamant that the pagan Greco-Roman texts should not be taught to children at all. Others decided they could be taught so long as the texts were carefully pruned of obvious pagan elements. One strategy was to cut and paste extracts, reformulating them to create Christian stories, or *centoni*. The papacy was, of course, highly suspicious of the flowering of interest in the pagan classics. In 1468, Pope Paul II ordered the suppression of the Roman Academy and the arrest and imprisonment of several of its members on charges of political conspiracy, sodomy, and the restoration of ancient pagan ceremonies.

The Academy had been founded in the 1450s by Julius Pomponius Laetus, otherwise known as Guilio Sanseverino (1427–98), with the aim of encouraging the study of ancient Roman culture. Its members were made up of literary and scholarly humanists, quite a few of whom worked as papal secretaries. Despite the use of torture, no sufficient evidence was found to substantiate the charges, and so everyone was released. The Academy was restored under subsequent popes, two of whom, Pope Julius II and Pope Leo X, were onetime members. Despite the papal patronage, this later manifestation of the Academy still attracted charges of paganism, particularly from non-Italian commentators critical of the papacy and suspicious of the influence of the *curia* (Vatican administration). The Dutch humanist priest and satirist Erasmus (d. 1536) was one of the most notable critics. In a letter written in 1526, he referred to 'certain pagans at Rome who abhor all Germans'.

Renaissance fascination with antiquity led to an enthusiastic interest in ancient Egypt that stretched far beyond liberal intellectuals. Rome, the seat of the papacy, was home to several ancient Egyptian obelisks, the spoils of imperial conquest. By the 16th century, only one remained upright, though. Standing 83 feet tall, it had been brought from Heliopolis on the order of Emperor Caligula. Several 15th- and 16th-century popes had toyed with the idea of having it removed to the Piazza of St Peter's, but it was Pope Sixtus V who realized the project in April 1586, to much fanfare. The following September, at another grand ceremony, Sixtus exorcised and purified the obelisk and a cross was placed on top. It was a symbolic act demonstrating Christianity's victory over paganism, but at the same time drew attention to the achievements of the ancient Egyptians. The public success of the venture led the pope to resurrect other obelisks in the capital in a similar fashion.

The origins of the world

The Renaissance engagement with the writings of the ancient Greeks and Romans nevertheless led intellectuals down some tricky paths of inquiry. Perhaps the most fundamental was the reconsideration of the chronology of the world. Calculations based on the number of generations between Adam and Jesus, as enumerated in the Old Testament, had put the beginning of the world at around 4,000 years before Christ. This is, of course, a chronology still supported by millions of creationists today. But the works of Cicero, Pliny, Aristotle, Plato, and other Greco-Roman authors, mentioned people and events that apparently predated

Adam. This was not a new discovery. Churchmen had long felt the need to dismiss the histories provided in the pagan classics. During the Renaissance, though, scholars were more willing to take them seriously – if only to explain them away rather than dogmatically reject them. So ink was spilled elucidating how the dynastic genealogies of ancient Egypt were deceptive, and had been manipulated by the Egyptian priesthood – a group regularly accused of being the greatest of what we would now describe as 'spin doctors'. Yet, for some, the sensational new evidence emerging from the newly 'discovered' Americas supported those pagan sources that pushed back history beyond 4000 BC.

Were the Indians encountered by the explorers and conquistadors confirmation of the pagan histories, of the existence of a pre-Adamite age? One Renaissance scholar who thought so was the occult scientist Theophrastus Bombastus von Hohenheim (1493–1541), better known as Paracelsus (a reference to the ancient Roman medical encyclopaedist Aulus Cornelius Celsus). For Paracelsus, the existence of the American Indians and the African pygmies was clear evidence that:

> The children of Adam did not inhabit the whole world. That is why some hidden countries have not been populated by Adam's children, but through another creature . . . For God did not intend to leave them empty, but had populated the miraculously hidden countries with other men.

Aware, no doubt, of the heretical nature of such musings, Paracelsus acknowledged that they might have originated after the Flood after all, or in any case such peoples had no souls and were, therefore, irrelevant to Christian doctrine. Those who considered the issue certainly had to be very careful. Sir Walter Raleigh was denounced in some quarters as an atheist for reporting his knowledge of Native American antiquities and foundation myths, even though his influential *History* kept strictly within the biblical chronology. In a hugely controversial work propounding the pre-Adamite theory entitled *Men before Adam*, the French Calvinist theologian Isaac La Peyrère (1596–1676) wrote that it was confirmed by the 'records of the Aegyptians, Aethiopians, and Scythians, and by parts of the frame of the world newly discovered'. The book was burned in France and contributed to his arrest on a visit to the Netherlands. He subsequently converted to Catholicism. Until the science of geology in the 18th century slowly led to the scientific rethinking of the Creation, only a very small minority of intellectuals held pre-Adamite theories.

Enlightenment

According to the historian Peter Gay, the Enlightenment of the 18th century represented the 'rise of modern paganism'. His definition of paganism symbolizes the emergence of increasing anti-clerical, anti-Christian, rationalist tendencies, coupled with a second Renaissance in the sense of a renewed passion for the cultural and scientific world of Greco-Roman antiquity. Gay's thesis was a reaction to, and the catalyst for, endless debates over the definition, character, and legacy of the Enlightenment, which need not be summarized here. It is worth noting, though, that the 1700s was as much a time of religious debate, controversy, and spirituality as previous centuries. In England, accusations of 'Pagano-papism', in other words that Catholicism was born of and perpetuated ancient paganism, were voiced repeatedly. Conyers Middleton's *A Letter from Rome, Shewing an Exact Conformity between Popery and Paganism* (1729) went through several editions during the 18th century.

Towards the end of the 18th century, the rise of Romanticism encapsulated a renewed artistic and aesthetic fascination with the classical pagan world. Idealized imaginings of ancient nature worship provided a refreshing contrast to the medieval gloom that inspired the Gothic. The sons of the wealthy were enthused by the ancient monuments they saw in Greece and Rome during their Great Tours. In Britain, Edward Gibbon's six-volume *History of the Decline and Fall of the Roman Empire*, published between 1776 and 1788, illuminated the glory of the pagan Empire as never before, while also providing, at times, a withering assessment of organized Christianity. Ancient Egyptian religion seeped into the beliefs of some Freemasonic groups who believed that the origins of Masonry stretched back to the pyramid builders.

In France, Rousseau weighed Christian society against classical pagan society and found it wanting. Christianity, he thought, created wars between friends, whereas in the old pagan world, 'Far from men fighting for the Gods, it was – as in Homer – the Gods who fought for the men.' The great German poets Goethe and Johann von Schiller fell in love with the gods of Rome and Greece, and the harmonious beauty of the sacred groves and pools where they were worshipped. In Britain, the Romantic poets Wordsworth, and particularly Keats and Shelley, imbued the landscape with pagan enchantment. Their tone could be joyous and celebratory, and yet mournful at the divorce of modern religious worship from the natural amphitheatre in which the ancients expressed their devotion. That said, none of the great poets espoused the renewal of pagan worship as an organized religion. Wordsworth and Coleridge thought paganism 'outworn' and 'exploded' as a religious creed.

The druids were also given a Romantic makeover. While the old portrayal of them as a blood-thirsty priesthood persisted, poets gave them new personae as gentle, nature-loving pagan mystics. When it came to re-writing their history, however, the druids were realigned with the Judaeo-Christian tradition. For the Welshman Iolo Morganwg (1747–1826), founder of the modern bardic tradition, the druids were early adopters of a pure form of Christianity. Having survived the Romans, they were then persecuted by Roman Catholic missionaries. According to one of Morganwg's harshest critics, fellow Welshman Edward 'Celtic' Davies, the druids worshipped a female and a male deity, the sun god Hu and his consort the Great Mother. So far so pagan, but

Davies believed Hu was, in fact, based on a distant memory of the biblical Noah.

Pagan survivals

As we saw earlier, 16th-century intellectuals speculated on the antiquity of the non-Christian beliefs and customs encountered by explorers and missionaries. In the second half of the 19th century, thanks to Darwin's theory of evolution, the 'pagan' beliefs and practices found overseas attracted a new and far-reaching significance. The new academic discipline of anthropology was much concerned with understanding the history of religion with regard to what it indicated about the development of society. Darwin's evolutionary model provided a template for how human *culture*, as well as human biology, had developed. So theories were conceived of a linear evolution of culture from savagery to civilization.

A three-stage model of progress proved popular. This mapped out how societies began in an age of magic before progressing to the development of organized religion, and then finally to the age of science, at which, it was confidently thought, Western European society had now arrived. The proof of this evolutionary model of religion was to be found in the present. The many 'primitive' cultures encountered in the far-flung territories of the British, French, and German empires provided a huge source material for understanding the first stage of the evolutionary model, that of savagery and magic. The sensational archaeological finds being reported from sites around the Mediterranean were testimony to the birth of the second stage, the age of religion.

It was also argued that there was another vital source of evidence only a horse-ride away from the very doorsteps of the middle-class homes of the European anthropologists and folklorists – the uneducated rural poor. As the influential classicist and social anthropologist James Frazer (1854–1941) advised, every inquiry into primitive religion should either start from the superstitious beliefs and observances of the peasantry, or should at least be constantly checked and controlled by reference to them. Compared with the evidence afforded by living tradition, the testimony of ancient books on the subject of early religion is worth very little.

Similarities could be found between the customs and beliefs of the European peasantry and those found in ancient myth and the 'savage' tribes of Asia, Africa, and the Americas. The conclusion was that they must all come from a common origin in the earliest stages of society. The illiterate rural poor were walking time capsules, their beliefs mental artefacts of an archaic primitive world. This was not an entirely new conclusion; 17th- and 18th-century antiquarians had described the 'superstitions' of the common people as mental 'vestiges', 'relics', and 'remains' akin to the physical remains of the ancient past such as stone circles and burial mounds. The English antiquary John Aubrey (1626–97), in his collection of traditions *Remaines of Gentilisme and Judaisme* reported, for example, the common children's rhyme against rain:

> Raine, raine, goe away,
> Come againe a Saterday

He believed that 'this childish custome is of Great antiquity; it is derived from ye Gentiles'. As we have seen earlier, 'gentile' had long been used to describe pre-Christians and pagans in the early Christian world.

But it was not until the development of anthropological theories of cultural evolution that this notion of the survival of decayed primitive belief into the present became a key to unlocking the progress of humankind. Its most influential proponent was the anthropologist Edward Burnett Tylor (1832–1917), whose book *Primitive Culture* (1871) set all sorts of folkloric hares running. Once people started looking, survivals of archaic pagan beliefs and practices started turning up everywhere. They could be found in practically every village in Britain and Europe. As the folklorist T. F. Thiselton Dyer explained in 1885:

> a great proportion of the superstitious usage that for centuries were observed throughout England, and many of which still linger on in remote districts, have an origin far older than Christianity itself. Introduced into the country from various sources and by different races, these pagan customs were often skilfully ingrafted into our Christian ceremonies.

Enthusiasm for decoding the pagan meaning of popular customs preoccupied many amateur folklorists and led to some surprising findings. In England, it was proposed, for example, that the tradition of eating hot-cross buns at Easter could be traced back to cakes eaten in honour of the Anglo-Saxon goddess Eostre. The rough-and-tumble parish football scrum played out on Old Christmas Day in Haxey, Lincolnshire, and the similar custom of Cornish hurling, became examples of 'ancient solar ritual'. It was widely believed in folklore circles in the early 20th century that morris dancing derived from a tradition of ancient pagan ritual combat. In the 1880s, a student of Greek folk songs came to the conclusion that they demonstrated that nearly 2,000 years of Christianity had 'hardly any effect even in modifying Pagan ideas and sentiments among the Greek folk'. The English folk-song collector Lucy Broadwood (1858–1929) thought she could discern pagan origins in many of the folk songs and dances she recorded.

Finding evidence of sacrifice was particularly satisfying. Numerous popular magical and medical practices were now explained away as survivals of this archetypal pre-Christian practice. So the folklorist who reported a cure for epilepsy in Ross-shire Scotland which involved the burial of a live black cock commented that it was, 'I suppose, a survival of old pagan sacrificial rites.' The colourful August 'Burry-man' festival in South Queensbury, Scotland, in which a boy dressed in a white flannel suit covered in burrs and a headdress of flowers, was interpreted in 1908 as 'a relic of an early propitiatory harvest rite … the modern form of the sacrifice required to ensure a fruitful season'. In 1907, a district medical officer reported how in Norfolk dairy workers would customarily milk a few drops onto the floor before milking into the pail. They said that they did this to clear the teat of any impurities that might spoil the milk. The medical officer, who was obviously grounded in folklore theory, read much more into the practice, though. It 'was clearly a survival of the rite of sacrifice, a libation poured upon the ground to propitiate the gods'. Norfolk having been part of the Danelaw during the Viking era, it was suggested the dairying practice might have been associated with a Scandinavian deity such as Freyja.

The folklorists exhibited a sense of wish-fulfilment. To record supposedly ancient customs and beliefs before they disappeared in the face of the inexorable march of progress and modernity was a worthy aim. The apparent breaking of a last link with our primitive past was a cause of sadness. Communities were seduced by the folkloric notion of pre-Christian survivals as it provided a comforting sense of being rooted in time immemorial. So there was and is a willingness to re-interpret and re-invent festivals as pagan vestiges when there may be no verifiable link at all. One example of this is the New Year's Eve 'fire festival' at Allendale in northern England. Central to the celebration is the carrying of burning barrels. This 'time-honoured custom', which some in the local community in the mid-20th century believed to be of pre-Christian origin, actually dated back only to 1858. The burning of the barrels was introduced to help light the open-air, nighttime Methodist hymn services conducted on New Year's Eve.

The most well-known case of the re-invention of a tradition to give it a pagan heritage is the Up-helly-aa festival in Lerwick, capital of the Shetland Islands, which today attracts thousands of visitors in January. It is likely that simple winter festivities involving music and dancing had carried on in Lerwick for centuries, just as they had elsewhere across Europe, but many of the 'ancient' aspects of Up-helly-aa are the products of 19th-century developments. The burning of tar barrels seems to have been introduced in the early 19th century. Concerns over public safety caused by this practice, and the drunkenness that accompanied such celebrations, led in the late 19th and early 20th centuries to a complete re-invention of the festival inspired by Shetland's Viking heritage. A 'pagan' Viking pageant was devised involving an ordered torch-lit procession by hundreds of men singing an 'ancient' song written in 1897, and the spectacular burning of a Viking-style longship as a sacrifice. Local socialists and the temperance movement also influenced the development of the pageant. It was all a long way from Norse pre-Christian religion.

Similar examples of the deliberate or unwitting generation of pagan interpretations of customs can be found elsewhere in Europe. Swiss and German folklorists have noted how sometimes even a basic investigation of historical sources reveals that many supposedly age-old traditions are of relatively recent date. One example is the well-attended *Perchtenlauf* Advent custom in the Bavarian village of Kirchseeon, which, like Up-helly-aa, was a deliberately invented calendar festival, this time introduced around 1954. The fancy wooden masks worn by participants, which portray demonic and beastly beings, were neither ancient nor local. The accompanying jumping up and down in a circle while jingling bells was soon being interpreted as the vestige of an ancient sun-rite. And so 'fakelore' became folklore.

Now, there certainly are traces of our pagan past to be found in the folklore of modern Europe. In Britain, one need only consider the days of the week and months named after pagan deities. But the enthusiastic search for survivals generated many misunderstandings. As the eminent historian of British paganism Ronald Hutton has discussed, 19th- and 20th-century calendar customs are survivals, but the 'Old Religion' they reflect is 'not a putative one concealed in the shades of pagan antiquity, but a well-documented one which was brought to an end only four to five centuries ago'. In other words, the ritual world of medieval Catholicism in a country that became Protestant in the 16th century.

Finding the first religion

The urge to re-interpret many popular customs as survivals of ancient sun worship and sacrifice owes much to two influential late 19th-century theories that claimed to reveal the existence of a single, original religion common to all humanity – a religion that could be described as pagan. The German philologist and Oxford don Max Müller (1823–1900) inspired the first of these theories. He was an expert on ancient Indian culture and its Sanskrit literature. His reading of the Sanskrit Vedic texts, the oldest written sources of Hinduism, led him to believe that he had found a direct connection between the names of ancient Indian gods and those of European pagan deities. His interpretation of these names and their linguistic usage led him to propose that the worship of the rising sun was the origin of all myth-religion. This solar mythology fed into and from the growing interest in the idea of a prehistoric Indo-European or Aryan (from the Sanskrit) culture, fragments of which survived in the languages, myths, histories, and archaeology of Europe, Persia, and India. This common ancestral culture was thought to be the source of the first civilizations.

The theory of solar worship as *the* foundation religion was pretty much dropped by academics after Müller's death, but by this time it had seeped into the consciousnesses of the numerous amateur folklorists looking for survivals and the means of decoding their significance. As solar worship waned in scholarly circles, the grand theory of a universal Old Religion was reworked. Inspired by the comparative approach and the theory of survivals, the 'myth-ritualists' believed that there was an inextricable link between ancient myths and primitive rituals – usually sacrificial ones. There was hardly unanimous agreement over the form of this relationship, though. The biblical scholar William Robertson Smith (1846–94), who pioneered myth-ritualist theory, thought that myth arose to explain ancient rituals once the original reason for conducting them had been lost. In Edward Burnett Tylor's view, however, myth came first and the meaning of ritual depended on the existence of myth.

The most influential of the myth-ritualists was James Frazer, whose work *The Golden Bough* was the most imaginative and exciting exercise in dot-joining survivalism. At the heart of the book (and its beginning and end) is the interpretation of an ancient Roman myth concerning the woodland sanctuary of the goddess Diana by Lake Nemi, formed in the crater of an extinct volcano situated around 15 miles south of Rome. Piecing together various classical references to the worship of Diana at Nemi revealed that the sanctuary was guarded by the *Rex Nemorensis*. This was a king or priest whose tenure in charge was only as long as he could prevent rivals from taking a bough from one of the sacred trees, for then he would have to engage his challenger in combat to the death. In Frazer's grand myth-ritual, this story, which he embroidered to fit his own needs, was interpreted as a classical manifestation of a far older universal religion based on fertility and renewal through the sacrifice of kings. In the most primitive stage of human society, the principal deity was the god of vegetation. The animating spirit of this god resided in a human sacred ruler. As long as this king was strong and healthy, so the land remained fertile. If the king weakened, so did the natural harvest. Then the king had to be killed and a new human vessel found for the vegetation god. He was, in essence, sacrificed to ensure the health of the god. Frazer believed he had found echoes of this old religion in myths and 'primitive' beliefs from around the globe, from the past and present. The story of Christ even fitted the pattern of divine sacrifice and renewal.

The numerous editions of *The Golden Bough* had an influence and popularity far beyond academia. It went through four editions between 1890 and 1922, and many more in the following decades. For some, it was a profound work, the key to humanity. At another level, it was a fascinating tour of the myriad 'savage' cultures of the British Empire. The fact that, as subsequent scholars have shown, there is little ethnographic, documentary or archaeological evidence for the widespread practice of ritual regicide of ailing kings has done little to dent its wider appeal. It continues to sell in large numbers today. That said, it has been remarked that it competes with *Das Kapital* and the *Origin of Species* in the list of unread modern classics. Its influence lies in the way it has been re-interpreted and used by other scholars, writers, and artists. One of those whom we now need to consider was Margaret Murray.

Margaret Alice Murray (1863–1963) was a respected Egyptologist at University College London and an enthusiastic supporter of Frazer's ideas. In 1914, she wrote an article in the anthropology journal *Man*, entitled 'Evidence for the Custom of Killing the King in Ancient Egypt'. Her opening sentence encapsulated perfectly the problem with the Frazerian approach: 'In Egypt there is no absolute direct evidence, no definite statement in so many words, that the king was sacrificed, no actual representations in sculpture or painting of such a sacrifice. Yet ...' What follows, of course, is an exercise in imagination. She creatively linked 'many allusions, more or less clear' to fit the theory for which the hard evidence was otherwise lacking. It was a scholarly approach that would lead to her own sensational findings regarding the survival of an ancient fertility 'witchcraft' cult in early modern Europe.

The idea that those accused of and executed for witchcraft in medieval and early modern Europe were the persecuted representatives of a female pagan fertility cult was developed in the mid-19th century by the French historian and romantic radical

Jules Michelet (1798–1874). For Michelet, this orgiastic 'witch cult', which worshipped a male fertility god, was an inspirational radical protest against a cruel, misogynistic, and oppressive medieval Church. In the 1890s, a new spin was put on Michelet's idea by the American journalist and Europhile Charles Leland (1824–1903), who was, like Murray, a member of the Folklore Society. In his *Aradia: Gospel of the Witches* (1899), Leland claimed that while in Italy studying the folk magic of its people he came across rumours of a book called the *Vangel* that contained the secrets of an ancient witchcraft religion. He managed to get hold of a copy that he thought was probably a translation from a medieval Latin manuscript. This 'Gospel of the Witches' revealed that its adherents were descendants of an ancient Etruscan cult of Diana.

It is easy to cast doubt on all this with hindsight, but considering the vogue for the scholarly theory of survivals, at the time it sounded quite feasible. It certainly did to Margaret Murray. She was no doubt influenced by Leland's *Aradia* and, through it, Michelet's notion of a witch cult. In 1921, her own book on the existence of the 'old religion' appeared, *The Witch-Cult in Western Europe*, published by Oxford University Press. From a literal reading of confessions (whether extracted by torture or otherwise), particularly those from Scotland, which she obtained from printed sources, she came to the conclusion that those tried as witches were secret followers of a fertility religion dating back to Palaeolithic times. They formed themselves into covens of thirteen and worshipped a phallic horned god. Each coven was led by a man (interpreted as the Devil in the confessions) who impersonated this god and who would let himself be sacrificed to ensure the fertility of the crops if need be. In subsequent books, *The God of the Witches* (1933) and *The Divine King in England* (1954), she reached for more and more disparate linkages between legend, folklore, archaeology, and historic events, to make increasingly far-fetched claims. So, according to Murray, Joan of Arc and

Thomas à Becket had been sacrificed to ensure the renewal of divine kingship and therefore fertility.

The fundamental flaws in Murray's thesis and research methods were clearly evident to some at the time and are to any historian today, but *The Witch-Cult in Western Europe* was widely embraced for decades by those folklorists, anthropologists, and historians who had imbibed the theory of survivals. The folk-song collector Lucy Broadwood, for instance, thought Murray's witch cult unlocked the secret to a number of 'old' English songs. They 'may be connected with the Witch Cult that Miss Murray proves to have been rampant, so late as the latter part of the seventeenth century', she wrote. Murray's theory was even absorbed into the work of Christopher Hill, the Marxist historian and Oxford don whose publications on 17th-century England were hugely influential in the 1960s and 1970s. The seal of approval on Murray's theory was provided by the invitation to contribute to the entry on witchcraft for the *Encyclopaedia Britannica*, which was published without alteration between 1929 and 1969.

Empire, Aryanism, and Nazism

Europe's perception of the Far East was changing by the end of the 19th century. The scholarly strands of sympathy regarding Eastern religions that had been fostered in the mid-19th century by Romantic respect, Orientalist scholarship, and notions of shared Indo-European heritage began to unravel. There was a reversion back to the racist model of Western superiority and Asian backwardness, inspired now by imperialist arrogance and scientific notions of racial evolution. The shift is most stark in the work of Jan de Groot (1854–1921), a Dutch professor of ethnology and a leading Sinologist in his day. Early in his career, he viewed China as a civilization comparable with Europe, and was attracted to its ancient religions. By 1912, he attacked China as 'the principal idolatrous and fetish-worshipping country in the world'.

The concept of Aryanism also became a vehicle for nationalistic and racist ideologies. The discussion of an Aryan *culture* turned into the definition of an Aryan *race* defined as superior to Semitic peoples. The European branch of this notional Aryan race also came to assume superiority over its Asian cousins. Perhaps the Aryan civilization had spread eastwards from Europe to India rather than the other way round? It was an idea that certainly suited India's British ruling class. Then, through further dubious studies of archaeology and myth, northern Europe came to be seen as the centre of the Aryan race. All sorts of theories were devised about the Nordic location of this lost Aryan heartland. Some called it Thule, and equated it with the legends regarding Atlantis. This fuelled the increasing influence of the German *völkisch* movement, which, with hindsight, can be defined as a racialist and nationalist wing of folklore studies. Germany had only come into existence as a modern nation state in 1871, and as with the forging of other newly formed states in Europe, history, myth, and folklore were important elements of the cultural cement that defined its identity, and rooted it in a noble past. Non-Germans also promoted the racialist concept of Aryanism, such as the British author Houston Stewart Chamberlain (1855–1927), who married into the Wagner family.

While this Aryan past was mostly framed within a Christian context, there were those who sought to identify and restore a pagan German religion. One of them was the Viennese writer and occultist Guido von List (1848–1919), who claimed to have identified the pagan sun-worshipping religion of the 'Aryo-Germans', a religion that he called Armanism. He further claimed to have discovered the secrets of the runes that were central to their faith. Willibald Hentschel (1858–1947) proposed the setting up of an Aryan Utopia called *Mittgart*, or Middle Earth, one of the realms mentioned in Norse mythology. The utopia would be

12. *Thor's Battle with the Giants* (1872), by the Swedish artist
Mårten Eskil Winge (1825–96), who produced a series of paintings
depicting Norse mythology. There was a vogue for such subject matter
at a time of swelling Norwegian and Swedish cultural nationalism

founded under the auspices of the Aryan god Artam and would ideally contain 1,000 women and 100 men. All sexual activity would be controlled by a communal leadership. In 1933, the Dutch-German historian Herman Wirth (1885–1981) published what he claimed was an ancient north German chronicle, the *Ura-Linda-Chronik*, which purportedly dated to the 3rd century BC. Heralded as a sensational pagan record of Nordic Aryan cosmology, it was nothing more than a forgery concocted in the 19th century.

Interest in such Aryan ideas and schemes circulated amongst the various racist nationalist groups that influenced the genesis of the Nazi party. The adoption of the swastika, which was understood to be a key Indo-European symbol, was one expression of this influence. Some historians have made reference to 'Nazi pagans' with regard to the religious views of the likes of the head of the SS Heinrich Himmler, the general Erich Ludendorff, and the Nazi racial theorist Alfred Rosenberg (1893–1946). Yet the fundamental religious position of leading Nazi esotericists was essentially Christian. Himmler rejected Catholicism but was sympathetic to Protestantism as a German-inspired religion. It was essential, of course, to argue that Jesus was an Aryan and not Semitic. Similarly, in his influential book *The Myth of the Twentieth Century* (1930), Rosenberg argued for the awakening of a new faith, but made it clear he was not proposing the restoration of an extinct religion. While certainly anti-clerical, he believed that Christianity could be cleansed of Jewish influence and he drew upon German medieval Christian mysticism.

The Third Reich was no friend to occultists and mystical groups, though. The former were eventually rounded up and the latter suppressed. Bernhard Rust, Reich Minister of Science and Education, kept a close eye on *völkisch* scholars in German universities to ensure they did not promote pagan tendencies. Hitler certainly had no time for research idealizing the prehistoric German past or fantasies of Aryan religions. He wrote in *Mein Kampf*:

The characteristic thing about these people is that they rave about old Germanic heroism, about dim prehistory, stone axes, spear and shield, but in reality are the greatest cowards that can be imagined. For the same people who brandish scholarly imitations of old German tin swords, and wear a dressed bearskin with bull's horns over their bearded heads, preach for the present nothing but struggle with spiritual weapons, and run away as fast as they can from every Communist blackjack.

Chapter 6
Return of the old gods

As outlined in the last chapter, there was a lot of talk about paganism in the 19th century, but always as a memory, survival, or abstract idea. It was one thing to study, reconstruct, and romanticize a pagan past, but no one was actually converting or reverting to paganism in the West even if they rejected Christianity. The term 'neo-paganism' had been used to describe Renaissance humanists, 18th-century religious sceptics, and Victorian pre-Raphaelite artists, but it was only in the 20th century that a truly new paganism emerged in Europe. For the first time in history, people began to identify themselves as pagans and the faiths they followed as pagan. Paganism was no longer only a definition of the 'other' but an expression of the self. In this context, Pagan requires a capital P. Let us begin with an examination of how this came about.

Occult revival

Previously we saw how the theory of survivals had helped generate the idea that remnant European pre-Christian religions had survived into the modern age, kept alive through what the authorities denounced as witchcraft and magic. While folklorists and anthropologists looked for evidence of this indigenous paganism in the rural communities of Europe, another path to a pagan past was being forged in middle-class British and French homes. The learned occultists of the second half of the 19th century were not particularly interested in the ritual survivals encoded in the customs of Europe's labouring poor, or the 'pagan' practices of the so-called 'savage' tribes of Africa. They were inspired by the sensational archaeological discoveries being made regarding magic and religion in the Hellenic world, and by the venerable religions and mystical belief systems found in Europe's Asian empire.

Other social and religious developments watered the seeds of Western esotericism and the new paganism it inspired. In mid-19th-century Britain, there was a discernible estrangement from the established churches amongst certain sections of educated society, and similar tendencies can be found in Catholic France too. The revelatory, providential, and mystical aspects of Christianity had been largely leached out of mainstream orthodox worship. This explains why in both countries spiritualism was received with such enthusiasm in the parlour rooms of the middle classes. Table-turning and table-rapping communications with the spirits of the dead were, for the adherents of spiritualism, clear proof of the fundamental basis of Christianity – of all religion for that matter: the existence of the afterlife. For others, though, spiritualism was the work of the Devil. It was not the dead who came knocking but Satan and his minions, who were ever trying to fool people into straying from true faith. Furthermore, this public enthusiasm for communing with the dead, whether real or diabolic, was also interpretable as a corrupting throwback to the ancestor worship of the ancient pagans.

The Theosophical Society was, perhaps, the most influential outgrowth from spiritualism as it developed from parlour-room pastime into a religious movement. At one time or another, most occultists were members. It was founded in 1875 by the followers of the Russian émigré Helena Petrovna Blavatsky (1831–91). In her well-travelled search for universal wisdom, Blavatsky had explored ancient religions, Kabbalah, Renaissance Christian occultism, and spiritualism, but her final path to enlightenment led to the 'Aryan' mystic truths held by the holy men of India and Tibet. The keys to unlocking universal religion lay not in the West but in the teachings of Hinduism and Buddhism.

Theosophy was a melting pot of religious elements from West and East, but ultimately the vast majority of theosophists were at heart Christians who found wisdom in the teaching of other religions. The same applies to Blavatsky, who explained in a private letter:

> People call me, and I must admit I call myself, a heathen. I simply can't listen to people talking about the wretched Hindus or Buddhists being converted to Anglican Phariseeism or the Pope's Christianity; it simply gives me the shivers. But when I read about the spread of Russian Orthodoxy in Japan, my heart rejoices.

But what Theosophy promoted was openness to non-Christian religions past and present. Her book *Isis Unveiled*, as the title suggested, deferred to the wisdom of ancient Egypt, though she believed that the pyramid builders were descended from Indian colonizers.

All these influences are evident in the teachings and membership of the Hermetic Order of the Golden Dawn, the first modern occult organization dedicated to the practice of ritual magic in Britain. Founded in 1888, the Golden Dawn never numbered more than a few hundred at most, and lasted just over a decade before splintering: it would, however, have a huge influence on 20th-century Western paganism. Its initiation structure and hierarchy were based on Freemasonry, and its rituals and magical philosophy were rooted primarily in Judaeo-Christian esotericism. The latter was interpreted as being, in part, derived from ancient Egypt. Ancient Greco-Egyptian magical rituals, as reconstructed from the recently deciphered papyri and inscriptions, were also important in shaping Golden Dawn rituals. Instead of lodges, as in Freemasonry, the Golden Dawn founders set up 'temples' dedicated to Egyptian gods. So there was the Isis-Urania temple in London, the Horus temple in Bradford, the Osiris temple in Weston-super-Mare, and the Amen-Ra temple in Edinburgh. Now, while this may sound like a full-blooded restoration of organized ancient paganism, most Golden Dawn members were not pagan worshippers. The majority considered themselves as adherents of a Christian mystic tradition that sought spiritual enlightenment, like Theosophists, through an exploration of the universality of religious experience and practice.

A few Golden Dawn members did step well beyond the Christian pale though. One of the Golden Dawn founders, Samuel Liddell MacGregor Mathers (1854–1918), expressed polytheistic notions of worship. It was Mathers who, in 1898, initiated Aleister Crowley into the London Isis-Urania temple. Crowley (1875–1947) was an unsettling influence, in part because of his violently anti-Christian views, which can easily be traced to his upbringing in the conservative, evangelical Plymouth Brethren. Crowley attracted national notoriety in the early 20th century for his various sexual and narcotic magical activities, which he introduced to others through his leadership of the British branch of a German ritual magic group called the Ordo Templi Orientis (OTO).

Although Crowley said he aimed 'to bring oriental wisdom to Europe and to restore paganism in a purer form', he never made fully clear in his writings his conception of the nature of this paganism. He was certainly a polytheist, rooted his cosmology in Hellenic syncretic religion, recognized Hebraic demonology, and considered himself as a prophet of the Egyptian god Horus. Indeed, in 1920 he founded the short-lived Abbey of Thelema (Greek for 'will') in Sicily in order to herald the new aeon of the god. The Italian Fascists were not sympathetic and expelled him three years later. There are numerous magical groups and individuals today who use Crowley's writings, *The Book of the Law*, in particular, as the basis for their rituals and cosmologies. Crowley's incorporation of Tantric sex into his worship appeals

13. Samuel Liddell MacGregor Mathers dressed in ritual
Egyptian-style garb for a performance of his recreation of the
rites of Isis

to some, while for modern Thelemites it is the guiding principle
of 'Do what thou wilt shall be the whole of the law'. His teachings
have also inspired the 'Left Hand Path' system of spiritual ritual
magic, or *magick* – the k is important to the self-definition of

modern practitioners. But modern ritual magicians do not necessarily consider themselves as pagans, and so I shall pass on to other developments.

Wicca

Crowley had a big influence on the man who would devise the most widely known expression of neo-paganism: Wicca or modern witchcraft. Gerald Gardner (1884–1964) spent much of his working life in the Far East, retiring from his last job as a customs official in Malaya in 1936. He returned to England, where he devoted his time to his archaeological, anthropological, and religious interests. He was a spiritualist, freemason, and a druid, and became a member of the OTO and the Folklore Society. He immersed himself in the writings of Crowley and was a fervent admirer of Murray and her theories. It is from such sources that he wove an account of how one night, in 1939, he had been initiated into a witches' coven in the New Forest. These witches had kept alive the pre-Christian fertility religion described by Margaret Murray in her *Witch Cult in Western Europe*. Even if the coven existed, it was no more than the recent creation of others who were inspired by the same sources. According to Gardner, the ancient secret rituals of the witches had been preserved in a precious manuscript known as the *Book of Shadows*. As Gardner's own copy, which he produced in the late 1940s, and later printed versions show, its contents derived from much more recent sources. It clearly owes a lot to the instructional texts of the Golden Dawn and Crowley's OTO, to several grimoires translated and printed by Mathers and Crowley, and to the spells and ideas contained in Charles Leland's *Aradia*. From this basis, the discovery of a continuous pre-Christian religion in England and the possession of a founding text, Gardner set about creating his own order of pagan witchcraft.

No matter the depth of Gardner's deception and invention in creating Wicca – and many contemporary adherents now accept

14. Gerald Gardner, founder of the Wiccan religion. His goatee beard and shock of snowy white hair were distinctive aspects of his carefully crafted image

he was at least economical with the truth – Gardner spawned the development of a vibrant new pagan religion that would, over the next few decades, generate numerous variants and pathways under the umbrella of 'witchcraft'. It is important to stress, though, that Wicca and other similar expressions of neo-paganism cannot be entirely divorced from the Judaeo-Christian sources that define both our understanding of the pagan past and inspired the magical texts that are the basis for many of the rituals used. That said, as pagan witchcraft attracted the public gaze from the 1960s onwards, poor journalism and Christian groups were responsible for promoting the pernicious and erroneous notion that Pagans were linked to Satanism and acts of anti-Christian desecration.

As the leading historian of paganism Ronald Hutton observed, 'the unique significance of pagan witchcraft to history is that it is the only religion which England has ever given the world'. Wicca and other modern witchcraft traditions spread across the English-speaking world as the counter-culture movement developed during the 1960s and 1970s. In America, some Gardnerian Pagans sifted through the early history of European colonization looking for signs that the old witchcraft religion had emigrated to the country along with the Puritans and traders. Were those executed at Salem members of the early modern witch cult identified by Murray? The early American colonist Thomas Morton (d. 1647), leader of the colony of Merry Mount, Massachusetts, was also identified as a Pagan pioneer. This was because he had enthusiastically promoted May Day celebrations as a unifying communal celebration involving local Native Americans. Puritans denounced as idol worship the setting up of a maypole as part of the festivities. No smoke without fire, thought some Wiccans. American Pagan witches showed much greater sensitivity about appropriating Native American religious traditions, while at the same time identifying affinities between the two, particularly with regard to the veneration of the natural world.

The more recent recognition of Wicca by the American visual media has also led to the global teen witch phenomenon that has troubled evangelical Christian groups. Television series such as

Buffy the Vampire Slayer, *Charmed*, and *Sabrina the Teenage Witch* normalized the idea of Wiccan magic for tens of millions of viewers, though without really portraying Wicca as a pagan *religion* as distinct from a mere source of spells. Still, through such programmes, Wicca has become the gateway to youthful exploration of paganism more generally.

Shaping national identity

While a minority of Western Europe's middle classes, alienated from orthodox Protestant and Catholic Christian worship, indulged in the religions of the Hellenic world and the East, others looked much closer to home. As revelations about divine kings, sacrifice, and witch cults played on the Western imagination, other notions of paganism swirled in the political winds that blew across Europe in the late 19th and early 20th centuries.

The Austro-Hungarian Empire sprawled across numerous ethnic 'nations' which expressed their independent stature through pride in the antiquity of their histories and cultures. Czech, Slovene, Slovak, Serb, Romanian, Croat, Bosnian, Hungarian, and Polish folklorists looked to rural folk customs and beliefs to piece together ethnic traditions traceable back to a past free of the histories of conquest and subjugation. Sometimes these histories stretched back to pre-Christian times. So the identification of apparent survivals of Hungarians' nomadic past, or Romanians' proud Roman-era Dacian ancestry, was particular appreciated. The late 19th century was also a time when the creation of a pan-Slavic cultural identity in Eastern Europe played a hugely important role in the power politics that contributed to the First World War. Then, in the aftermath of the war, new countries were formed across eastern and northern Europe and their intellectuals looked back to an ancient past to define their nations' ethnic pre-Christian identity.

Norway and Estonia could be used to illustrate these developments, but Lithuania makes for a particularly interesting example. As we saw in Chapter 3, Romuva (Romowe) was, according to the 14th-century Teutonic chronicler Peter von Duisburg, the location of a great sacred site presided over by a high priest who guarded a sacred flame. This sole report was then embellished in the 16th century by the Catholic priest Simon Grunau in his colourful and fanciful history of Prussia. This is the sum of evidence for the existence of Romuva, whose name suspiciously derives from 'Rome'. Grunau's history first appeared in print in the late 19th century, and as a result Romuva began to attract increased popular curiosity. At the same time, a huge collection of 'archaic' Lithuanian folk songs, or *dainas*, some of which apparently preserved pre-Christian myth and belief, was also published.

The philosopher, theosophist, and Lithuanian nationalist Vilius Storostas-Vydūnas (1868–1953) wrote a play, performed in 1912, in which the story of Romuva was idealized. Other romantics also saw in its sacred flames a symbol of the eternal spirit of the Lithuanian people. Vydūnas was not arguing for a restoration of paganism, but it was an idea that was attractive to some of those trying to create a coherent Lithuanian cultural identity following the restoration of sovereign nationhood after the First World War. A similar development took place in neighbouring Latvia during the 1920s where folk songs and folklore inspired the founding of the Dievturi movement, which promoted the revival of pre-Christian 'traditional' religion. The Soviet invasion in 1940 effectively put an end to such nascent movements.

In the late 1960s, as signs of liberal cultural expression began to manifest elsewhere in the Eastern Bloc, the legend of Romuva was once again resurrected as a national symbol, and in 1967 the new Romuva movement celebrated the summer solstice. Further festivals were arranged, though in 1971 the authorities arrested the organizers. With the collapse of the Soviet Union and the

restoration of Lithuanian independence in 1990, Romuva
followers were given new freedoms, and a pagan altar was built
in the capital Vilnius. In 2003, they numbered between 1,000
and 3,000, less than 1% of the population, but nevertheless their
existence has meaning for many more in the country. Branches
of Romuva have also been founded amongst Lithuanian
communities in the United States, Canada, and Australia.

Let us turn now to the other end of the former Eastern Bloc to
consider another example of the re-appropriation of pagan identity
for nationalist purposes, but one that had more profound and
bloody global significance. An ecclesiastical report submitted to the
archiepiscopal assembly of the Serbian Orthodox Church in 1996,
warned of the 'brutal and uncompromising re-paganization of
Serbia'. Its authors saw this as a satanic exercise in destabilizing
Serbia's youth, fuelled by a pernicious foreign New Age
movement. But Serbia's own nationalism had also promoted a
romantic re-assertion of its heroic pre-Christian past. This had its
roots in the independence movement of the late 19th and early
20th centuries, when the south Slavic sun and war god Vid became
a significant component in the mythologizing of the Battle of
Kosovo. The battle happened in 1389. The Ottomans defeated the
Serbian forces and Serbia was reduced to a vassal state. Although
there were other equally crucial military engagements in the
struggle between the two sides, Kosovo became the focus of
Serbian national memory.

The battle took place on 28 June under the old Julian calendar
followed by the Orthodox Church. This was also 'Vidovdan', the
day dedicated to St Vitus, or St Vit in Serbian. St Vitus was a
Sicilian who was martyred in AD 303, but 19th-century Serbian
folklorists and historians believed that his place in Serbian culture
was due to his having been adopted as a Christianized version of
the god Vid after the conversion of the Serbians in the 9th century.
As elsewhere, survivals were sought for the god in Serbian
folklore in order to prove the continued worship of the war god

in the guise of St Vitus. Having made the connection between the two, the promotion of St Vitus in conjunction with the Battle of Kosovo now had an important new meaning for Serbian national identity and the country's rebirth. Until the second half of the 19th century, the Orthodox Church did not formally celebrate Vidovdan, but the nationalist promotion of Vid/Vitus led to its inclusion in Church calendars from the 1860s onwards. Following the 500th anniversary of the Battle of Kosovo, popular support swelled for making Vidovdan a national holiday. This was instituted in 1914 following a successful war against Turkish forces the previous year. As people across the country celebrated the new holiday, the Bosnian Serbian nationalist Gavrilo Princip carried out his plan to assassinate Archduke Franz Ferdinand.

Writing in 1976, when Serbia was part of communist Yugoslavia, the historian Miodrag Popović warned:

> The cult of St. Vitus's day, which combines historical reality with myth, a real fight for freedom with pagan tendencies... potentially has all the characteristics of a milieu with untamed mythical impulses. As a phase in the development of national thought, it was historically indispensible. However, as a permanent state of mind, the St. Vitus cult can be fatal for those who are not able to free themselves from its pseudo-mythical and pseudo-historical snares.

Prophetic words. With the disintegration of Yugoslavia in the early 1990s and the wars between the various constituent parts, Serbian politicians once again promoted the Kosovo/Vidovdan myth as a rallying banner for a military campaign under the auspices of the heroic past against ancient enemies. The celebration of the 600th anniversary of the Battle of Kosovo on Vidovdan was a display of how folklore and mythologizing about the past could be put to destructive racial and martial purposes.

Following the collapse of the Soviet Union, Paganism and 'Native Faith' groups sprang up in Russia, Ukraine, Slovakia, Belarus, and elsewhere as people looked to restore national religions free of the Communist and Orthodox past. Political and racial ideologies run deep in these recent Eastern European expressions of neo-Paganism. Some groups, such as the Slavic Pagan Movement, have overtly right-wing nationalist tendencies, and others are vehemently anti-Christian. In 1996, the Orthodox Cathedral in Minsk was desecrated with graffiti proclaiming 'Christians, go away from our Belorussian soil'. As with the founding of Wicca, numerous Slavic Pagan groups have been inspired by the amazing modern discovery of a text claiming to have ancient origins. The *Book of Veles* purports to be a medieval chronicle written on wooden plates, which describes the early history of the Slavs and the pre-Christian religion they followed. There are references to the worship of the deities Triglav, Perun, Svarog, and Svetovid, amongst others. The *Book of Veles* is almost certainly a forgery dating to the 1940s. As with the *Book of Shadows*, though, it has transcended its dubious genesis.

The old and the new

Pretty much every historic form of paganism described in this *Very Short Introduction* now has a contemporary manifestation, no matter how little source material there is to work on to reconstruct forms of worship. There are numerous expressions of pagan Celtic faith, which draw inspiration from medieval accounts of the myths of Ireland and Wales. Another attraction is the swirling artistic designs found on prehistoric monuments and artefacts, and Christian crosses and illuminated manuscripts, which are given the very broad description of 'Celtic art'. The Vikings are represented by 'Heathen' groups such as the Odinic Rite, founded in Britain in the 1970s, and the Rune-Gild, whose members describe themselves as the followers of the 'Path of Odin'. In Norway, heavy metal music provides a major outlet for expressions of Norse Paganism, with subgenres being labelled Viking Metal and Pagan Metal.

Shamanism has become one of the most popular forms of Paganism. Traces of shamanic practices are enthusiastically sought in pretty much every corner of Europe in the attempt to restore 'ancestral paths' to the earliest religions. Claims have been made for shamanic elements in the Icelandic sagas and eddas, and in the sources regarding 'Celtic' Irish religious practices. Survivals have also apparently been discerned in the records of the 17th-century Scottish witch trials. The desire to seek shamanism everywhere is an aspect of a strong theme in modern Paganism, that of a universal pagan worldview. This is based on the identification of core concepts of ancient worship, such as the localized manifestation of deities and spirits, and the emphasis on ritual performance over dogma and belief. These values can be found in archaic and modern forms, and underpin diverse religions across the world such as Shinto, Hinduism, and the indigenous religions of Australia and Africa. This conception of global similarities takes us back to the definition of paganism used in the religious surveys of the early 19th century, except this time it is not a derogatory label but a positive act, the recognition of paganism's value and influence in the world.

One important unifying theme from a global Pagan perspective, and one which has huge contemporary resonance, is respect for the environment as a spiritual entity. The term 'earth-centred religions' is used to express this. We have seen how the early Church associated paganism with nature worship, and that this was a fairly accurate attribution. Gods were worshipped as natural features, such as trees, rocks, or springs, or all of nature was imbued with animistic properties. The destruction of the environment, the cutting down of trees and groves, the polluting of water, were acts of desecration. Today, this conception of the natural environment as intrinsically sacred is shared by neo-Pagans and indigenous religions across the globe. Common

15. Adherents of modern witchcraft performing a ritual 'skyclad', or naked. Ritual nudity is most associated with Gardnerian Wicca, but it is also practised by other Pagan groups and individuals

cause and shared identity are forged in an awareness of ecological degradation and the need to protect the natural world, whether it be Uluru (Ayers Rock) in Australia, the rain forests of South America, or the chalk downlands of southern England. The green message is also enshrined in the prominence that some modern Pagans give to the universal conception of an earth goddess, or Gaia in ancient Greek religion. The personification of life-giving earth as a female deity is a powerful and emotive symbol that contrasts with the male-dominated and human preoccupation of the major monotheisms.

Comparing the new Paganisms with the old religions we have explored through the archaeological record, and the Greco-Roman and early Christian literature, we of course find similarities, since many neo-Pagans look to the same scant sources for inspiration. But there are differences too. Idol worship, particularly in the form

of wooden poles and columns, is not exactly a common modern
practice. One might also ask: 'Where's the sacrifice?' This was
clearly a fundamental part of all forms of paganism identified in
the past. Modern Heathen groups place more emphasis than
others on the value of blood sacrifice, or *blót*, but most offer wine in
lieu of blood or feast on a supermarket roast. Pretty much all
other Pagan faiths reject animal sacrifice outright. There are
pragmatic reasons for rejecting blood sacrifice in modern Western
society, such as health and safety laws. But the vast majority of
Pagans find it repulsive for ethical reasons. I suspect that Pagans
are significantly more likely to be vegetarian than the general
public. Of course, as we have seen, blood sacrifice was by no
means the only form of sacred offering in the past. Furthermore,
the importance of blood sacrifice was, in part, predicated on the
fact that domesticated animals, along with weapons, were the most
valued of possessions, and therefore represented considerable
personal sacrifice.

While some Wiccans, and the members of other modern Pagan
faiths, continue to cling to the notion that they are part of a
continuous tradition of pre-Christian worship, others feel that
their paganism need not be tied to traditions or histories. For
some, paganism encapsulates the freedom to explore multiple
faiths, old and new, and from across the globe, including
Christianity. Numerous contemporary Pagans, after
experimenting with the likes of Wicca, settle on pursuing an
individual spiritual path that subscribes to monotheism as well
as polytheism. The sociological notion of 'believing without
belonging', which has usually been used in relation to
contemporary Christian faith, is now equally pertinent to
Paganism.

The term 'Pagan' has become increasingly problematic in recent
years. This takes us back to the issues of definition raised in the
Introduction. There are people who might be described as neo-
Pagans in terms of their beliefs and practices in relation to both

past and present conceptions of the term, but who reject such an identity. This could spring from an awareness of its historic Christian definition. It could be because they have a monotheistic faith and associate paganism with polytheism. Some find it inappropriate because they have drawn upon aspects of Christianity. Most of all, perhaps, 'Pagan' has become problematic once again because people tend to reject labels that attempt to define their personal belief systems, which are often organic and changing, depending on their spiritual needs and life experiences.

In contemporary society, Paganism can be a liberating spiritual and social force, but can also manifest as a facet of racial and religious intolerance. As a concept, it is no less relevant than it was when it was redefined by Christians nearly two millennia ago. It has retained its ability to stimulate intellectual curiosity and spiritual exploration. Paganism always has been an expression of the imagination, and it continues to excite.

References

Introduction

On the definition and origin of the term 'pagan', see: Robin Lane
    Fox, *Pagans and Christians in the Mediterranean World from the
    Second Century to the Conversion of Constantine* (London, 1986);
    Pierre Chuvin, *A Chronicle of the Last Pagans*, tr. B. A. Archer
    (Cambridge, Mass., 1990); J. J. O'Donnell, '"Paganus": Evolution
    and Use', *Classical Folia*, 31 (1977): 163–9; Maijastina Kahlos,
    Debate and Dialogue: Christian and Pagan Cultures c. 360–430
    (Aldershot, 2007).
Wolfram Drews, 'Jews as Pagans? Polemical Definitions of Identity
    in Visigothic Spain', *Early Medieval Europe*, 11 (2002): 189–207.
Thomas Abernethie, *Abjuration of poperie* (Edinburgh, 1638), p. 28.
Frank R. Trombley, *Hellenic Religion and Christianization, c. 370–529*
    (Leiden, 1993), part 1, p. x.
Roger Beck, 'Four Men, Two Sticks, and a Whip: Image and Doctrine
    in a Mithraic Ritual', in *Theorizing Religions Past: Archaeology,
    History, and Cognition*, ed. Harvey Whitehouse and Luther H.
    Martin (Walnut Creek, 2004), p. 88.

Chapter 1

Paul G. Bahn, *Prehistoric Rock Art: Polemics and Progress* (Cambridge,
    2010).
R. Dale Guthrie, *The Nature of Paleolithic Art* (Chicago, 2005).
Neil S. Price (ed.), *The Archaeology of Shamanism* (London, 2001).
On prehistoric and ancient religion, see, for example, Harvey
    Whitehouse and Luther H. Martin (eds.), *Theorizing Religions*

Past: Archaeology, History, and Cognition (Walnut Creek, 2004); John R. Hinnells (ed.), *A Handbook of Ancient Religions* (Cambridge, 2007); Garry Trompf, *In Search of Origins: The Beginnings of Religion in Western Theory and Archaeological Practice* (New Delhi, 1990).

Stephen Mitchell and Peter van Nuffelen (eds.), *One God: Pagan Monotheism in the Roman Empire* (Cambridge, 2010).

Polymnia Athanassiadi and Michael Frede (eds.), *Pagan Monotheism in Late Antiquity* (Oxford, 1999).

T. D. Barnes, 'Monotheists All?', *Phoenix*, 55 (2001): 142–62.

Manfred Clauss, *The Roman Cult of Mithras: The God and His Mysteries*, tr. Richard Gordon (Edinburgh, 2000).

Roger Beck, *The Religion of the Mithras Cult in the Roman Empire* (Oxford, 2006).

On Neoplatonism and paganism, see Ronald Hutton, *Witches, Druids and King Arthur* (London, 2003), ch. 5; Polymnia Athanassiadi, 'Persecution and Response in Late Paganism: The Evidence of Damascius', *Journal of Hellenic Studies*, 113 (1993): 1–29; W. Den Boer, 'A Pagan Historian and His Enemies: Porphyry against the Christians', *Classical Philology*, 69 (1974): 198–208.

For a meticulous account of pagan practices in European antiquity, see Ken Dowden, *European Paganism: The Realities of Cult from Antiquity to the Middle Ages* (London, 2000).

Jan N. Bremmer (ed.), *The Strange World of Human Sacrifice* (Leuven, 2007).

Miranda Green, *Dying for the Gods: Human Sacrifice in Iron Age and Roman Europe* (Stroud, 2001).

Scott Bradbury, 'Julian's Pagan Revival and Blood Sacrifice', *Phoenix*, 49 (1995): 331–56.

Maijastina Kahlos, *Debate and Dialogue: Christian and Pagan Cultures c. 360–430* (Aldershot, 2007), pp. 119–23.

Dennis D. Hughes, *Human Sacrifice in Ancient Greece* (London, 1991).

Donald G. Kyle, *Spectacles of Death in Ancient Rome* (London, 1998).

J. Rives, 'Human Sacrifice among Pagans and Christians', *Journal of Roman Studies*, 85 (1995): 65–85.

Maria-Zoe Petropoulou, *Animal Sacrifice in Ancient Greek Religion, Judaism, and Christianity, 100 BC to AD 200* (Oxford, 2008).

Miranda Green, *Animals in Celtic Life and Myth* (London, 1992), ch. 5.

John Fotopoulos, *Food Offered to Idols in Roman Corinth* (Tübingen, 2003).

J. B. Rives, 'The Decree of Decius and the Religion of the Empire', *Journal of Roman Studies*, 89 (1999): 135–54.

On idol worship, see, for example, Dowden, *European Paganism*; Ton Derks, *Gods, Temples, and Ritual Practices: The Transformation of Religious Ideas and Values in Roman Gaul* (Amsterdam, 1998), chs. 4 and 5.

Harry A. Hoffner, 'Oil in Hittite Texts', *The Biblical Archaeologist*, 58, 2 (1995): 108–14.

Stephen Benko, *Pagan Rome and the Early Christians* (Bloomington, 1984).

James B. Rives, 'The Blood Libel against the Montanists', *Vigiliae Christianae*, 50 (1996): 117–24.

Chapter 2

Ramsay MacMullen, *Christianizing the Roman Empire* (New Haven, 1984).

Robin Lane Fox, *Pagans and Christians* (London, 1986).

Garth Fowden, 'The Pagan Holy Man in Late Antique Society', *Journal of Hellenic Studies*, 102 (1982): 46–8.

Garth Fowden, *The Egyptian Hermes: A Historical Approach to the Late Pagan Mind* (Princeton, 1993).

Pierre Chuvin, *A Chronicle of the Last Pagans*, tr. B. A. Archer (Cambridge, 1990).

James J. O'Donnell, 'The Demise of Paganism', *Traditio*, 35 (1979): 45–88.

For religious persecution in Antioch, see J. H. W. G. Liebeschuetz, *Decline and Fall of the Roman City* (Oxford, 2001), pp. 241–3.

Stephen McKenna, *Paganism and Pagan Survivals in Spain up to the Fall of the Visigothic Kingdom* (Washington, 1938).

On Caesarius of Arles, see Yitzhak Hen, *Culture and Religion in Merovingian Gaul, AD 481–751* (Leiden, 1995).

John Blair, *The Church in Anglo-Saxon Society* (Oxford, 2005).

Doron Bar, 'The Christianisation of Rural Palestine during Late Antiquity', *Journal of Ecclesiastical History*, 54, 3 (2003): 401–21.

On the growth of religious establishments along the Mediterranean, see Peter Brown, *The Rise of Western Christendom: Triumph and Diversity, AD 200–1000* (Oxford, 1996), p. 221.

Richard Fletcher, *The Barbarian Conversion: From Paganism to Christianity* (Berkeley, 1999).

On paganism in Turkey, see Frank Trombley, 'Paganism in the Greek
World at the End of Antiquity: The Case of Rural Anatolia and
Greece', *Harvard Theological Review*, 78, 4 (1985): 327–52.

Vasilios Makrides, *Hellenic Temples and Christian Churches: A Concise
History of the Religious Cultures of Greece from Antiquity to the
Present* (New York, 2009).

On Christian uses of pagan sites in late antiquity: Jason Moralee,
'The Stones of St. Theodore: Disfiguring the Pagan Past in Christian
Gerasa', *Journal of Early Christian Studies*, 14, 2 (2006): 183–215;
Helen Saradi-Mendelovici, 'Christian Attitudes toward Pagan
Monuments in Late Antiquity and Their Legacy in Later Byzantine
Centuries', *Dumbarton Oaks Papers*, 44 (1990): 47–61.

Sarah Semple, 'A Fear of the Past: The Place of the Prehistoric Burial
Mound in the Ideology of Middle and Later Anglo-Saxon England',
World Archaeology, 30, 1 (1998): 109–26.

Howard Williams, 'Monuments and the Past in Early Anglo-Saxon
England', *World Archaeology*, 30, 1 (1998): 90–108.

John Blair, *The Church in Anglo-Saxon Society* (Oxford, 2005).

Richard Morris, *Churches in the Landscape* (London, 1989).

K. W. Harl, 'Sacrifice and Pagan Belief in Fifth- and Sixth-Century
Byzantium', *Past and Present*, 128, 1 (1990): 7–27.

Frank Trombley, *Hellenic Religion and Christianization c. 370–529*
(Leiden, 1993), vol. 1.

Jitse H. F. Dijkstra, 'A Cult of Isis at Philae after Justinian?:
Reconsidering P. Cair. Masp. I 67004', *Zeitschrift für Papyrologie
und Epigraphik*, 146 (2004): 137–54.

On the city of Harran, see Tamara M. Green, *The City of the Moon God:
Religious Traditions of Harran* (Leiden, 1992); Ronald Hutton,
Witches, Druids and King Arthur (London, 2003), pp. 138–52;
Jaako Hämeen-Anttila, 'Continuity of Pagan Religious Traditions
in Tenth-Century Iraq', in *Ideologies as Intercultural Phenomena*,
ed. A. Panaino and G. Pettinato (Milan, 2002), pp. 89–108.

Dorothy Watts, *Religion in Late Roman Britain* (London, 1998), p. 50.

For the problems regarding the archaeological evidence for pagan
survival, see John Blair, *The Church in Anglo-Saxon Society*
(Oxford, 2005); Sally Crawford, 'Votive Deposition, Religion and
the Anglo-Saxon Furnished Burial Ritual', *World Archaeology*, 36
(2004): 87–102; Edward James, 'Burial and Status in the Early
Medieval West', *Trans Royal Historical Society*, 39 (1989): 23–40;
Martin Carver (ed.), *The Cross Goes North: Processes of Conversion
in Northern Europe, AD 300–1300* (Woodbridge, 2003).

Michele R. Salzman, '"Superstitio" in the Codex Theodosianus and the Peresecution of Pagans', *Vigiliae Christianae*, 41 (1987): 172–88.

S. A. Smith and Alan Knight (eds.), *Religion of Fools? Superstition Past and Present* (Oxford, 2008).

Valerie Flint, *The Rise of Magic in Early Medieval Europe* (Princeton, 1991).

Edward Peters, 'The Medieval Church and State on Superstition, Magic and Witchcraft from Augustine to the Sixteenth Century', in *Witchcraft and Magic in Europe: The Middle Ages*, ed. Bengt Ankarloo and Stuart Clark (London, 2001), pp. 173–246.

Bernadette Filotas, *Pagan Survivals, Superstitions and Popular Cultures in Early Medieval Pastoral Literature* (Toronto, 2005).

Chapter 3

D. H. Green and F. Siegmund (eds.), *The Continental Saxons: From the Migration Period to the Tenth Century* (Woodbridge, 2003).

Ian Wood, *The Missionary Life: Saints and the Evangelisation of Europe 400–1050* (Harlow, 2001).

On the Stellinga, see Ruth Mazo Karras, 'Pagan Survivals and Syncretism in the Conversion of Saxony', *Catholic Historical Review*, 72 (1986): 558.

Nora Berend (ed.), *Christianisation and the Rise of Christian Monarchy: Scandinavia, Central Europe and Rus c. 900–1200* (Cambridge, 2007).

Josef Poulik, 'The Origins of Christianity in Slavonic Countries North of the Middle Danube Basin', *World Archaeology*, 10, 2 (1978): 158–71.

Leszek Paweł Słupecki, *Slavonic Pagan Sanctuaries*, tr. Izabela Szymańska (Warsaw, 1994).

Roman Zaroff, 'Perception of Christianity by the Pagan Polabian Slavs', *Studia Mythologica Slavica*, 4 (2001): 81–96.

'faithful Teutonic Catholics ...' cited in F. L. Carsten, 'Slavs in North-Eastern Germany', *Economic History Review*, 11, 1 (1941): 66.

Cornelius J. Holtorf, 'The Life-Histories of Megaliths in Mecklenburg-Vorpommern (Germany)', *World Archaeology*, 30, 1 (1998): 23–38.

On the evidence of worship at Slavic temples, see R. Pettazzoni, 'The Pagan Origins of the Three-Headed Representation of the Christian Trinity', *Journal of the Warburg and Courtauld*

Institutes, 9 (1946): 135–51; Roman Zaroff, 'The Origins of Sventovit of Rügen', *Studia Mythologica Slavica*, 5 (2002): 9–18; http://christianization.hist.cam.ac.uk/regions/poland/poland-pagan-non-christ.html, accessed 26 November 2010.

Anders Andrén, Kristina Jennbert, and Catharina Raudvere (eds.), *Old Norse Religion in Long-Term Perspectives* (Lund, 2006).

Thomas Andrew DuBois, *Nordic Religions in the Viking Age* (Philadelphia, 1999).

Peter Buchholz, 'Aspects of Recent Research in Pagan Germanic and Scandinavian Religions', in *The Notion of 'Religion' in Comparative Research*, ed. Ugo Binachi (Rome, 1994), pp. 383–95.

P. H. Sawyer, *Kings and Vikings: Scandinavia and Europe, AD 700–1100* (London, 1982), p. 131.

Stefan Brink, 'Law and Legal Customs in Viking Age Scandinavia', in *The Scandinavians from the Vendel Period to the Tenth Century: An Ethnographic Perspective*, ed. Judith Jesch (Woodbridge, 2002), pp. 87–117.

Birgit Sawyer, *The Viking-Age Rune-Stones: Custom and Commemoration in Early Medieval Scandinavia* (Oxford, 2000).

Mindy MacLeod and Bernard Mees, *Runic Amulets and Magic Objects* (Woodbridge, 2006).

Anders Andrén, 'Behind *Heathendom*: Archaeological Studies of Old Norse Religion', *Scottish Archaeological Journal*, 27 (2005): 105–38.

Lars Larsson, 'The Iron Age Ritual Building at Uppåkra, Southern Sweden', *Antiquity*, 81 (2007): 11–25.

Gavin Lucas and Thomas McGovern, 'Blood Slaughter: Ritual Decapitation and Display at the Viking Settlement of Hofstaðir, Iceland', *European Journal of Archaeology*, 10 (2007): 7–30.

John Blair, *The Church in Anglo-Saxon Society* (Oxford, 2005).

Dawn Hadley, '"Cockle amongst the Wheat": The Scandinavian Settlement of England', in *Social Identity in Early Medieval Britain*, ed. William O. Frazer and Andrew Tyrrell (London, 2000), pp. 128–30.

James Graham-Campbell and Colleen Batey, *Vikings in Scotland* (Edinburgh, 1998), p. 48.

Richard A. Fletcher, *The Barbarian Conversion: From Paganism to Christianity* (New York, 1998), p. 388.

On Irish pre-Christian religion, see Dáithi Ó hÓgáin, *The Sacred Isle: Belief and Religion in Pre-Christian Ireland* (Woodbridge, 1999); Kim McCone, *Pagan Past and Christian Present in Early Irish*

Literature (Maynooth, 1990); Ronald Hutton, *Blood and Mistletoe* (Yale, 2009), ch. 1.

Lesley Abrams, 'The Conversion of the Scandinavians of Dublin', *Anglo-Norman Studies*, 20 (1997): 1–29.

Vykintas Vaitkevičius, 'The Sacred Groves of the Balts: Lost History and Modern Research', *Electronic Journal of Folklore*, 42 (2009): 81–94.

Jonė Deveikė, 'The Legal Aspect of the Last Religious Conversion in Europe', *Slavonic and East European Review*, 32 (1953): 117–31.

S. C. Rowell, *Lithuania Ascending: A Pagan Empire within East-Central Europe, 1295–1345* (Cambridge, 1994).

Giedrė Mickūnaitė, *Making a Great Ruler: Grand Duke Vytautas of Lithuania* (Budapest, 2006).

Heiki Valk, 'Christianisation in Estonia: A Process of Dual-Faith and Sycretism', in *The Cross Goes North: Processes of Conversion in Northern Europe, AD 300–1300*, ed. Martin Carver (Woodbridge, 2003), pp. 571–81.

Heiki Valk, 'Sacred Natural Places of Estonia: Regional Aspects', *Electronic Journal of Folklore*, 42 (2009): 45–66.

Chapter 4

Jerry H. Bentley and Herbert F. Ziegler, *Traditions and Encounters: A Global Perspective on the Past* (Boston, 2000).

Christopher Hodgkins, 'Stooping to Conquer: Heathen Idolatry and Protestant Humility in the Imperial Legend of Sir Francis Drake', *Studies in Philology*, 94, 4 (1997): 428–64.

Bruce G. Trigger, 'Early Native North American Responses to European Contact: Romantic Versus Rationalistic Interpretations', *Journal of American History*, 77, 4 (1991): 1195–1215.

Pedro Aguado quoted in Marion A. Habig, 'The Franciscan Provinces of South America', *The Americas*, 2, 2 (1945): 198.

Quotes from José de Anchieta are from Donald W. Forsyth, 'The Beginnings of Brazilian Anthropology: Jesuits and Tupinamba Cannibalism', *Journal of Anthropological Research*, 39, 2 (1983): 155–6.

Håkan Rydving, 'Saami Responses to Christianity: Resistance and Change', in *Beyond Primitivism: Indigenous Religious Traditions and Modernity*, ed. Jacob Olupona (London, 2003), ch. 5.

Ake Hultkrantz, 'Swedish Research on the Religion and Folklore of the Lapps', *Journal of the Royal Anthropological Institute of Great Britain and Ireland*, 85, 1/2 (1955): 81–99.

Michael Khodarkovsky, '"Not by Word Alone": Missionary Policies and Religious Conversion in Early Modern Russia', *Comparative Studies in Society and History*, 38 (1996): 267–93.

Paul W. Werth, 'Baptism, Authority, and the Problem of Zakonnost', in 'Orenburg Doicese: The Induction of over 800 "Pagans" into the Christian Faith', *Slavic Review*, 56, 3 (1997): 456–81.

Regarding the Canary Islands, see David Abulafia, *The Discovery of Mankind: Atlantic Encounters in the Age of Columbus* (New Haven and London, 2008), p. 47.

Red Jacket quote in Granville Ganter (ed.), *The Collected Speeches of Sagoyewatha, or Red Jacket* (Syracuse, 2006), p. 248.

1856 Foreign Missions quote in Robert F. Berkhofer, Jr, 'Protestants, Pagans, and Sequences among the North American Indians, 1760–1860', *Ethnohistory*, 10, 3 (1963): 204.

Ho-Fung Hung, 'Orientalist Knowledge and Social Theories: China and the European Conceptions of East–West Differences from 1600–1900', *Sociological Theory*, 21, 3 (2003): 254–80.

John Hayward, *The Religious Creeds and Statistics of Every Christian Denomination in the United States* (Boston, 1836), pp. 72, 76.

Robert Eric Frykenberg (ed.), *Christians and Missionaries in India: Cross-Cultural Communication since 1500* (Richmond, 2001).

Douglas M. Peers, *India under Colonial Rule 1700–1885* (Harlow, 2006).

Quote on the Hindus of Columbo from *The Panoplist, and Missionary Magazine* (Boston, 1817), p. 465.

David Ramsey, *Universal History Americanised*, vol. 2 (1819): 336.

The medical journal quote is from the *Dublin Journal of Medicine*, 12 (1838): 162.

Regarding the Dyaks, *Report of the American Board of Commissioners for Foreign Missions* (1839): 11.

Robin Law, 'Human Sacrifice in Pre-Colonial West Africa', *African Affairs*, 84, 334 (1985): 53–87; Olatunji Ojo, 'Slavery and Human Sacrifice in Yorubaland: Ondo, c. 1870–94', *Journal of African History*, 46 (2003): 379–404.

1819 report in *The Methodist Magazine* 14 (1821): 149.

H. Barth, 'A General Historical Description of the State of Human Society in Northern Central Africa', *Journal of the Royal Geographical Society of London*, 30 (1860): 122.

Vivian C. Hopkins, 'De Witt Clinton and the Iroquois', *Ethnohistory*, 8, 2 (1961): 113–43.

David Boyle, 'On the Paganism of the Civilised Iroquois of Ontario', *The Journal of the Anthropological Institute of Great Britain and Ireland*, 30 (1900): 263–73.

Chapter 5

Joscelyn Green, *The Pagan Dream of the Renaissance* (London, 2002).

James Hankins, *Humanism and Platonism in the Italian Renaissance* (Rome, 2003), vol. 1, p. 548.

Erasmus cited in Alexander Dalzell (ed.), *The Correspondence of Erasmus: Letters 1658 to 1801* (Toronto, 2003), p. 220.

On pre-Adamism, see David N. Livingstone, *Adam's Ancestors: Race, Religion, and the Politics of Human Origins* (Baltimore, 2008); Ernest A. Strathmann, 'Raleigh on the Problems of Chronology', *The Huntingdon Library Quarterly*, 11, 2 (1948): 129–48; Philip C. Almond, *Adam and Eve in Seventeenth-Century Thought* (Cambridge, 1999); Richard Henry Popkin, *Isaac La Peyrère (1596–1676): His Life, Work, and Influence* (Leiden, 1987).

Dorinda Outram, *The Enlightenment* (Cambridge, 1995).

Roy Porter, *The Enlightenment* (Basingstoke, 1990).

Peter Harrison, *'Religion' and the Religions in the English Enlightenment* (Cambridge, 1990), p. 144.

James Frazer, preface to first edition of *The Golden Bough* (1890).

Dyer quote from T. F. Thiselton Dyer, 'Superstition in English Life', *The North American Review*, 140 (1885): 468.

Stephen D. Corrsin, 'The Founding of English Ritual Dance Studies before the First World War: Human Sacrifice in India... and in Oxfordshire?', *Folklore*, 115 (2004): 321–31.

J. S. Stuart-Glennie, 'Folk-Lore as the Complement of Culture-Lore in the Study of History', *Folklore-Journal*, 4, 3 (1886): 213.

Sheila MacDonald, 'Old-World Survivals in Ross-shire', *Folklore*, 14, 4 (1903): 370.

Isabel A. Dickson, 'The Burry-Man', *Folklore*, 19, 4 (1908): 379–87.

On the Norfolk dairy ritual, *Folklore*, 18, 4 (1907): 436.

Venetia Newell, 'The Allendale Fire Festival in Relation to its Contemporary Social Setting', *Folklore*, 85, 2 (1974): 93–103.

Callum Brown, *Up-Helly-Aa: Custom, Culture and Community in Shetland* (Manchester, 1998).

References

Venetia Newall, 'The Adaptation of Folklore and Tradition (Folklorismus)', *Folklore*, 98, 2 (1987): 132.

Quote from Ronald Hutton, *The Stations of the Sun: A History of the Ritual Year in Britain* (Oxford, 1996), p. 416.

For an introduction to the historic scholarship on mythology, see Robert A. Segal, *Myth: A Very Short Introduction* (Oxford, 2004).

Mary Beard, 'Frazer, Leach, and Virgil: The Popularity (and Unpopularity) of the Golden Bough', *Comparative Studies in Society and History*, 34, 2 (1992): 203–24.

Joseph Fontenrose, *The Ritual Theory of Myth* (Berkeley, 1966).

M. A. Murray, 'Evidence for the Custom of Killing the King in Ancient Egypt', *Man*, 14 (1914): 17–23.

On Murray, see Caroline Oates and Juliette Wood, *A Coven of Scholars: Margaret Murray and Her Working Methods* (London, 1998).

A. G. Gilchrist and Lucy E. Broadwood, *Journal of the Folk-Song Society*, 7, 28 (1924): 174–83.

Jan de Groot quote in Ho-Fung Hung, 'Orientalist Knowledge and Social Theories: China and the European Conceptions of East–West Differences from 1600 to 1900', *Sociological Theory*, 21, 3 (2003): 268.

Stefan Arvidsson, *Aryan Idols: Indo-European Mythology as Ideology and Science*, tr. Sonia Wichmann (Chicago, 2006).

See Nicholas Goodrick-Clarke, *The Occult Roots of Nazism* (London, 1985).

James Webb, *The Occult Establishment* (La Salle, 1975).

Richard Steigmann-Gall, 'Rethinking Nazism and Religion: How Anti-Christian Were the "Pagans"?', *Central European History*, 36 (2003): 75–105.

Horst Junginger (ed.), *The Study of Religion under the Impact of Fascism* (Leiden, 2007).

Chapter 6

On the origins of modern pagan witchcraft, see Ronald Hutton, *Triumph of the Moon: A History of Modern Pagan Witchcraft* (Oxford, 1999).

Chas Clifton, *Her Hidden Children: The Rise of Wicca and Paganism in America* (Lanham, 2006).

Sabina Magliocco, *Witching Culture: Folklore and Neo-Paganism in America* (Philadelphia, 2004).

Tamas Hofer, 'The Perception of Tradition in European Ethnology', *Journal of Folklore Research*, 21 (1984): 133–47.

Tõnno Jonuks, 'Archaeology of Religion – Possibilities and Prospects', *Estonian Journal of Archaeology*, 9, 1 (2005): 32–56.

Audroné B. Willeke, 'Vydūnas' Dramas: A Ritual of National Salvation', *Journal of Baltic Studies*, 21, 4 (1990): 359–68.

Michael Strmiska and Vilius Rudra Dundzila, 'Romuva: Lithuanian Paganism in Lithuania and America', in *Modern Paganism in World Cultures: Comparative Perspectives*, ed. Michael Strmiska (Santa Barbara, 2005).

Michael Strmiska, 'The Music of the Past in Modern Baltic Paganism', *Nova Religio*, 8, 3 (2005): 39–58.

Olga Zirojević, 'Kosovo in the Collective Memory', in *The Road to War in Serbia: Trauma and Catharsis*, ed. Nebojša Popov and Drinka Gojković (Budapest, 2000), pp. 189–212.

Ivo Zanic, 'New Myths for Old', *Index on Censorship*, 4 (1999): 157–65.

Radost Ivanova, 'Once More about the Kosovo Epos and Its Utilization', *Ethnologia Balkanica*, 3 (1999): 181–95.

Mitja Velikonja, *Religious Separation and Political Intolerance in Bosnia-Herzegovina* (College Station, 2003), pp. 99–100.

Miodrag Popović quoted in Olga Zirojević, 'Kosovo in the Collective Memory', p. 201.

On the *Book of Veles*, see Adrian Ivakhiv, 'The Revival of Ukrainian Native Faith', in Strmiska (ed.), *Modern Paganism*.

On Slavic neo-paganism, see Adrian Ivakhiv, 'Nature and Ethnicity in East European Paganism: An Environmental Ethic of the Religious Right?', *The Pomegranate*, 7, 2 (2005): 194–225; Victor A. Shnirelman, '"Christians! Go Home": A Revival of Neo-Paganism between the Baltic Sea and Transcaucasia', *Journal of Contemporary Religion*, 17, 2 (2002): 197–211; Marlène Laruelle, 'Alternative Identity, Alternative Religion? Neo-Paganism and the Aryan Myth in Contemporary Russia', *Nations and Nationalism*, 14, 2 (2008): 283–301; Anne Ferlay, 'Neopaganism and New Age in Russia', *Electronic Journal of Folklore*, 23–4 (2003): 40–8.

Graham Harvey, 'Heathenism: A North European Pagan Tradition', in *Paganism Today*, ed. Graham Harvey and Charlotte Hardman (London, 1995), pp. 49–65.

Imke von Helden, 'Barbarians and Literature: Viking Metal and Its Links to Old Norse Mythology', in *The Metal Void: First Gatherings*, ed. Niall W. R. Scott (Oxford, 2010), pp. 257–64.

On shamanism past and present, see Ronald Hutton, *Shamans: Siberian Spirituality and the Western Imagination* (London, 2001); Robert J. Wallis, *Shamans/Neo-Shamans: Ecstasy, Alternative Archaeologies and Contemporary Pagans* (London, 2003); Alby Stone, *Explore Shamanism* (Loughborough, 2003).

On Paganism as a global religion, see Michael York, *Pagan Theology: Paganism as a World Religion* (New York, 2005).

Joanne Pearson, Richard H. Roberts, and Geoffrey Samuel (eds.), *Nature Religion Today: Paganism in the Modern World* (Edinburgh, 1998).

Adrian Harris, 'Sacred Ecology', in *Paganism Today*, ed. Graham Harvey and Charlotte Hardman (London, 2001), pp. 149–57.

Further reading

On pagan religions in the ancient world see: Ronald Hutton, *The Pagan Religions of the Ancient British Isles* (Oxford, 1991); Jack Finegan, *Myth & Mystery: An Introduction to the Pagan Religions of the Biblical World* (Grand Rapids, 1997); Ken Dowden, *European Paganism: The Realities of Cult from Antiquity to the Middle Ages* (London, 2000);); John R. Hinnells (ed.), *A Handbook of Ancient Religions* (Cambridge, 2007); Mary Beard, John North and Simon Price, *Religions of Rome*, 2 vols (Cambridge, 2008); Daniel Ogden (ed.), *A Companion to Greek Religion* (Oxford, 2007); Robert Parker, *Polytheism and Society at Athens* (Oxford, 2005).

Regarding the role of Christianity in usurping and defining pagan religions in late antiquity and the medieval period, Prudence Jones and Nigel Pennick, *A History of Pagan Europe*, 2 edn. (London, 2006) provides a useful basic survey from a modern practitioner slant. For more detailed scholarly analysis see: Robin Lane Fox, *Pagans and Christians in the Mediterranean World from the Second Century to the Conversion of Constantine* (London, 1986); Ramsay MacMullen, *Christianity & Paganism in the Fourth to Eight Centuries* (New Haven, 1997); Richard A. Fletcher, *The Barbarian Conversion: From Paganism to Christianity* (New York, 1998); Martin Carver (ed.), *The Cross Goes North: Processes of Conversion in Northern Europe, AD 300–1300* (Woodbridge, 2003); A. D. Lee, *Pagans and Christians in Late Antiquity: A Source Book* (London, 2000).

Christian encounters with indigenous religions in the age of exploration are examined in: David Abulafia, *The Discovery of Mankind: Atlantic Encounters in the Age of Columbus* (New Haven and London, 2008); Charles H. Parker, *Global Interactions in the Early Modern Age: 1400-1800* (Cambridge, 2010); Elizabeth Isichei, *A History of Christianity in Africa: From Antiquity to the Present* (London, 1995); Jerry H. Bentley and Herbert F. Ziegler, *Traditions and Encounters: A Global Perspective on the Past* (Boston, 2000).

The study of modern western Pagan religions has recently become an established aspect of historical, sociological and anthropological scholarship. Accordingly, a substantial body of literature is already accumulating. For overall surveys of Britain see Ronald Hutton's pioneering *Triumph of the Moon: A History of Modern Pagan Witchcraft* (Oxford, 1999); Leo Ruickbie *Witchcraft out of the Shadows: A Complete History* (London, 2004); Joanne Pearson, *Wicca and the Christian Heritage* (London, 2007). Regarding the USA see: Chas Clifton, *Her Hidden Children: The Rise of Wicca and Paganism in America* (2006); Sabina Magliocco, *Witching Culture: Folklore and Neo-Paganism in America* (2004); Margot Adler, *Drawing Down the Moon: Witches, Druids, Goddess-Worshippers, and other Pagans in America*, revised and updated (London, 2006). There is an even greater and ever expanding number of guides written by practitioners regarding the many forms that modern Paganism takes. For general introductions to the range of beliefs read Joanne Pearson, *A Popular Dictionary of Paganism* (London, 2002); Graham Harvey, *What do Pagans Believe?* (London, 2007); Barbara Jane Davy, *Introduction to Pagan Studies* (Plymouth, 2007); Chas Clifton and Graham Harvey (eds.), *The Paganism Reader* (London, 2004); Michael York, *Pagan Theology: Paganism as a World Religion* (New York, 2005).

Index

Index

Paganism

Expand your collection of
VERY SHORT INTRODUCTIONS